EinFach
Englisch

AF198529

Gran Torino

... verstehen

Edited by
Ulrike Klein
Gabriele Kugler-Euerle

westermann GRUPPE

© 2019 Bildungshaus Schulbuchverlage
Westermann Schroedel Diesterweg Schöningh Winklers GmbH, Braunschweig
www.westermann.de

Druck A^1 / Jahr 2019
Alle Drucke der Serie A sind im Unterricht parallel verwendbar.

Sprachliche Betreuung: Michelle R. Büscher
Umschlaggestaltung: Nora Krull, Bielefeld
Umschlagbild vorne/hinten: © Mark Wiener/Alamy Stock Foto
Druck und Bindung: Westermann Druck GmbH, Braunschweig

ISBN 978-3-14-**041296**-4

Contents

How to work with "EinFach Englisch *Gran Torino* verstehen"

Clint Eastwood, dir:
Gran Torino, Warner Bros 2008.

This study guide has been designed to deepen your individual understanding of the movie *Gran Torino*.
It provides you with …

- **information on the script, director and main actors**
- **plot summaries**
- **explanatory information on the setting and background**
- **character analyses**
- **aspects of a deeper analysis of the motifs and themes**
- **motivating ideas and useful vocabularies for your own text production.**

Stop-and-think tasks focus your attention on relevant points along the way and raise your awareness for the **language of film**.

Symbols guide you through your work with this booklet and clarify the various **functions of information and assignments**:

- the **information** is designed to help you understand particular aspects of the film within a larger context
- **assignments** ask you to reflect on your personal understanding of the movie, individual scenes or characters and help you process the extra information given
- sections marked by this symbol make you aware of how **the language of film** accentuates certain **motifs and themes** underlying the movie

We hope this study guide helps you enjoy this movie even more and we wish you lots of success in your work!

About this movie …

Students who have already studied this movie and were asked to write a review about it most frequently used the following key words:

▷ Study this graphic while listening to the movie's original theme song, "Gran Torino", which you can find online by using a streaming service.
With a partner discuss how you feel about the atmosphere created by the title song. Explain what in the graphic catches your interest? What aspect of the movie are you curious about?

Yet, films in general target audiences not only through their contents but also through the genre they belong to.

▷ Which genre do you expect? Collect information on the different formats and decide which genre you expect this movie to belong to.

The genre

Genres	are/depict
Action	• fast paced • physical stunts and chases • rescues, battles, fights, escapes, destructive crises • often one-dimensional heroes and villains *(good guy – bad guy)*
Adventure	• searches for the unknown • journeys to exotic locations • "jungle" and "desert" epics
Animated	• (not strictly related to genre but more to technique) • often designed to appeal most strongly to children • animals and/or usually inanimate objects become evil villains or heroes
Comedy	• light-hearted plots designed to amuse the audience and provoke laughter • exaggerated situations, language, action, relationships and characters • some different types: *slapstick, screwball, spoofs* and *parodies, romantic comedies, black comedy*
Crime	• fast paced with an air of mystery • actions of a criminal mastermind versus the rise and fall of sinister criminals
Documentary	• non-fictional • "slice of life" reporting on an issue of interest
Drama	• serious and plot-driven • real-life characters, settings, situations, and stories involving intense character development and interaction • strong human emotions • usually not focused on special effects

Genres	are/depict
Fantasy	• imaginative and fantastic themes • fairy-tale adventures or plots from the Dark Ages • magic, supernatural events
Horror	• large amount of violence and gore in the plot • arousal of the audience's worst fears and nightmares about the arrival of an evil force, person, or event • mythical creatures, such as ghosts, vampires, and zombies
Romance	• varying tone from happy to tragic • love between two protagonists, e. g. *love at first sight, forbidden love, love triangles, and love requiring great sacrifices*
Science Fiction	• hypothetical, science-based • outer-space adventures and extra-terrestrial encounters • futuristic elements and technological advances that raise important social, political, and philosophical issues • usually set in the future, either on Earth or in space
Suspense/ Mystery	• a person of authority, usually a detective, trying to solve a mysterious crime • clues, investigation, and logical reasoning • "whodunit" suspense created through visual cues or unusual plot twists

Before you now learn more about the contents of the movie, here are first of all the most basic facts about it.

Gran Torino – key data ⓘ

Release date: December 2008
Country: USA
Distributed by: Warner Bros. Pictures
Running time: 116 minutes
Language: English
Budget: $33 million
Box office: $270 million
Genre: Drama, Thriller
Cert (UK): 15
USA: Rated R for language throughout, and some violence
Germany: 12
Directed by: Clint Eastwood
Produced by: Clint Eastwood
Screenplay by: Nick Schenk
Starring: Clint Eastwood, Christopher Carley, Bee Vang, Ahney Her and others
Music by: Kyle Eastwood, Michael Stevens, Jamie Cullum

Approaching *Gran Torino*

Actually there is no best way to learn about a film. Sometimes it is through recommendation of friends, sometimes through a sneak-preview we catch at a cinema or the short glimpse of film advertising of an upcoming film that we hear and see in the media for the first time. And sometimes it can also be a film poster.

The film poster

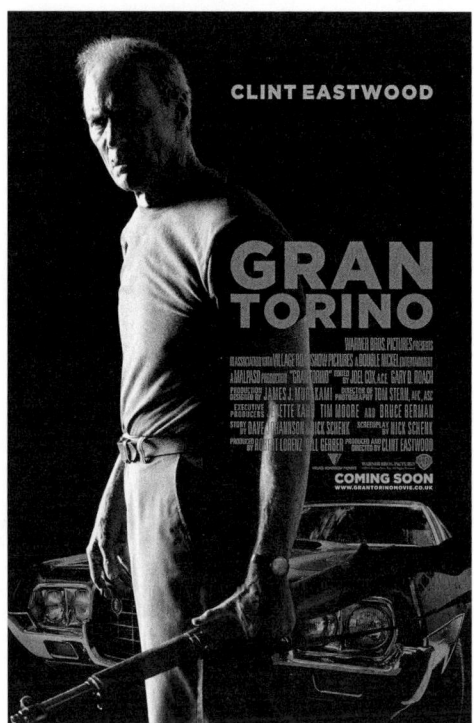

Film posters in general promote a film to be released soon by sparking the interest of potential audiences in **the genre, story line and main characters**. Additional information on the **production company, cast and crew** usually relate the upcoming movie to former box-office successes.

1▷ Study the promotional poster or DVD cover of the film *Gran Torino* and tick the relevant boxes to explain whether the poster adopts the general design of movie posters.

Film posters usually …

☐ feature the movie title prominently
☐ show the film's main actor(s)
☐ reflect the film's mood and tone through the colors used
☐ use details such as objects and symbols to make the audience speculate about the contents
☐ contain a memorable tagline

The effectiveness of a film poster depends on its eye-catching form: **images** and **graphics** to hint at the **genre** and **narrative**; **designs**, **colors** and **fonts** to reflect the **tone** and **atmosphere** of the film.

2▷ Rank the following observations on the right in the order you became aware of them and link them on the left to the message they send.

The film poster for *Gran Torino* aims to attract audiences who enjoy movies …

a) containing dramatic tension.

b) showing a male view of the world.

c) depicting the topic of protecting law and order, right and wrong.

d) focusing on one protagonist, powerful and ready to take on the enemy.

e) starring the famous actor Clint Eastwood.

f) dealing with the past.

☐ Contrasts and limited, dark colors dominate the poster.

☐ The sole images used: the silhouette of a man and details of a gun and a car.

☐ Eastwood's name is printed in bold capital letters in the top-right-hand corner of the poster.

☐ The character's silhouette is accentuated by low key lighting.

☐ Eastwood is shown with his typical squint, looking scornful at what is going on, straight down the camera.

☐ The character is depicted with a gun, implying Eastwood's typical image as a gun-wielding action hero.

☐ Only the title of the movie, at the center, is printed in color (orange).

☐ The car, depicted as a photo negative, is aligned to the right, as are the title and credits.

- [ ] For this poster, the medium shot of the character is taken from a low angle.
- [ ] The darkish colors of the credits and crew, blending into the background, keep the viewer's attention on the character and title.
- [ ] The gun can be identified as the standard US service rifle during World War II and the Korean War (M1 Garand); the car, a Ford Gran Torino, was produced in the 1970s.

▷ 3 ▷ Use the information above to write your individual analysis of the poster. Also use the vocabulary given in the following box.

Vocab: Film posters

Film posters	
Layout	<ul><li>detailed/simple</li><li>main focus of the layout is/the poster is split in two/the layout separates ... from .../the layout is well spread out/the layout places emphasis on</li><li>the edges are blackened/blurred</li><li>in the foreground/background/center/on the left/right/at the bottom/top of ...</li></ul>

Film posters	
Image	• key image/main image/the image in focus/the image taking up the most space • realistic/edited/focused/blurry/blocked • to depict/show/portray/represent/illustrate/convey
Colors	• black-and-white/colored/a color palette varying from … to … • realistic/surreal/edited • the colors contrast/emphasize/suggest/blend into one another/(sharply) separate … from …
Text	• title – credits – tagline/slogan – billing block (text at the bottom of a film poster giving more detailed information about the film and its cast and crew) • cast (all actors in a film or play) – crew (all the people involved behind the scenes in making a film or play) – director – producer • have the leading role/feature/star/act in a film • genre: drama/comedy/thriller/mystery/science fiction • positioned at the top/bottom/edge/on the right/left/in the center/dominate/be the focus of attention • in small/large lettering/font size – big/small/highly-condensed typeface – large/bold/italic type – capital letters
Viewer's reaction	• focus attention on/draw the eye to/divert/distract attention from/catch the viewer's interest/make the viewer focus on • make the viewer wonder why/believe/think/hope/fear • intrigue the viewer with/by/the viewer naturally assumes … • … suggest that/evoke a sense of …/signal to the viewer

The film

A first viewing of *Gran Torino*

After analysing the poster you obviously already have an idea of what the film will be about. Please state your expectations in five precise statements about the main characters, then verify these statements when you now watch the film.

- _____
- _____
- _____
- _____
- _____

▷ Having watched the film read the following summary of it. Illustrate the observations and analyses in **bold print** by using scenes from the film.

In the movie *Gran Torino*, Clint Eastwood plays the role of Walt Kowalski, an **embittered and lonely old man**, who hates sharing his neighborhood in the suburbs of Detroit with a majority of Asian families living next door. **Memories of a war** long past still **haunt Walt's world of today and** make him **despise the foreigners and their strange customs**. After the death of his wife and disillusioned when it comes to his sons and their families he seems to have **withdrawn from the com-**

pany of others and concentrates on **home repairs**, only sharing an **occasional beer with other veterans** or going on a **trip downtown to see his friend, the barber**. However, when **a gang brawl involving the boy from next door** spreads onto his lawn, he is suddenly confronted with the **realities of multiracial America in an urban community** where **different ethnicities and cultures** either lead **parallel lives** or **clash**. Walt cannot help **becoming involved in the worries of the neighboring family** and decides to mentor and coach young **Thao, who is putting his future on the line** when he nearly gives into **gang pressure**. Walt ends up **defending those in whom he once falsely saw the enemy of his past** and realizes that he is in fact **more closely connected to these people than to anyone else**.

Analysing contents and themes of the film

To start the analysis it is helpful to become focused. Having watched the movie and studied the plot summary above, there is now the question of which theme or motif dominates the movie.

 ▷ Here are some ideas. Tick the one which you personally find most convincing.

Gran Torino is about …

☐ a grumpy old man who overcomes his prejudice by helping his teenager neighbor.

☐ a disgruntled Korean War veteran, Walt Kowalski, who sets out to teach his neighbor, a Hmong teenager, about life and death.

- [ ] a Hmong teenager who tries stealing his white neighbor's 1972 Gran Torino and much to his surprise finds a friend for life in this cantankerous old man.

- [ ] a racist Korean War veteran who is forced to confront his racial prejudice when the neighboring Hmong family needs his help in fending off an Asian gang.

- [ ] an unlikely friendship between an old Caucasian war veteran and an Asian teenager who take on the challenge of peaceful co-existence in their mixed suburban neighborhood.

- [ ] a recently widowed old man, alienated from his sons and angry at the world, who finds a surrogate family in the Asian people next door.

- [ ] a heavily biased retired auto worker who becomes the hero of the neighborhood when he stands in the way of an Asian gang.

Scene-by-scene analysis

On the left, the following pages take you through the plot of all the scenes whereas …

Gran Torino or …

Gran Torino is a film about **family relations, racial tension, concepts of life, good and evil, and growing up and growing old in a complex world**. The American suburb serves as backdrop for a **21st century environment** in which people distinct in experience, culture and outlooks on life must learn to share their common space and come to terms with one another. The plot evolving around the two central characters – one Caucasian, the other Asian; one old and sure that he knows about life, the other young and lacking orientation – raises questions about what it takes for individuals to stand their ground and whether **mutual understanding and living together in a multi-ethnic community** is possible.

… the explanations **on the right** show how the central motif of the film is emphasized and expressed through twists in the plot, quotes of the characters and the language of film.[1]

… The Ambiguity of Belonging

When Walt Kowalski's self-inspection leads him to wonder why he has *more in common with his next-door neighbors than with his own spoiled-rotten family* he touches on the central motif of the movie. Although his detachment from his family, friends, and the church seems self-chosen, his remark shows that principally he sees man as part of something bigger than only himself and his act of self-sacrifice in the end is consequently aimed at making the world a better place for Thao and his family.

Psychologists and sociologists would agree and say that **a sense of belonging is a human need**, just like the need for food and shelter. Being accepted as a member or part of something, family, friends, an age or interest group, the social media, a culture or country, etc. is **essential for the well-being and healthy development of a person**, and for their **happiness**. The feeling of belonging and sharing common interests and aspirations but also problems or distress makes an individual **see value in life** and motivates people to **meet challenges** and **show persistence** in difficult times.

Belonging, however, does **also involve constraint and limitation** to a person's individual freedom. The demand

---

[1] On pages 55 and 57 (+ 59) you also find additional information on the car Gran Torino as well as on the use of racist language in the film.

Act One:

The set-up establishes the status quo of **Walt Kowalski**, the **complex central character, full of flaws**, who pursues a clear goal but is **confronted with a conflict**/a predicament that is central to the story and provides tension. At the end of Act One, Walt will be **propelled into a new direction** because backing out is no longer possible.

 ▷ Before reading the plot summaries use the expressions in bold print to retell the events yourself.

for **conformity** within a group and the necessity to continuously **comply with others** challenges a person to **balance their own needs or aspirations and the inclinations and aims of the other**. This process involves pain and frustration, which questions the obvious widening of perspective on things and the opportunity for personal growth. The key to individual development lies in that person's ability to **perceive others with empathy and compassion**, to realize that all people struggle and can fail, and to understand that acceptance and solidarity do not necessarily mean agreement. **Tolerance and mutual support** help to **overcome isolation, loneliness and despair**.

About Life and Death

The **motif of belonging** sets the plot of the movie in motion. Walt, as the central character of the movie, is introduced as impassive and detached. The reason for this lies not only in the grief over his wife's death but also in a defiant retreat from everyone and everything around him. He feels that life, his children, and his nation have failed him and he stubbornly believes that he is out there alone. Only reluctantly, because circumstances beyond his control force him to, Walt realizes that he and the people next door are in this together – they not only share the same neighborhood but also the challenge to forge their present and future together.

▷ In the analysis sections, highlight words and expressions that help you characterize the two protagonists.

The funeral service

The film opens on a scene in which **family and friends gather in church to pay their respects** to the wife of a grim looking, stony-faced elderly man, Walt Kowalski. Walt **scrutinizes** every move and disrespectful behavior on the part of his grandchildren and **shows open contempt** of the Catholic priest's eulogy on life and death. His family seems to show little regard for Walt's grief or the memory of their mother and grandmother.

Gran Torino. Dir. by Clint Eastwood. Actors (left to right): Christopher Carley, Brian Haley, Dreama Walker, Geraldine Hughes, Clint Eastwood. Warner Bros Pictures 2009.

In the opening scene, establishing shots and panning shots introduce the location of a church in which a funeral service is held and people pay their respect to the deceased. Then a zoom-in to medium shots and close-ups of an elderly man focus the viewer's attention on the main character.

Walt Kowalski is depicted looking around disgustedly at the congregation from which he seems isolated. Later he sits at a distance from his family as can be seen in the picture above. No physical contact, no interaction. The short dialogue between his sons characterizes Walt as a relic from the 1950s, intransigent and grumpy, difficult to be around. Mirroring the sons' words, Walt's eyes narrow with disdain at the inadequate dress and behavior of his grandchildren. His facial expression, solemn and unresponsive at first, quickly betrays his obvious contempt for the people around him, his family, the mourners and also the young priest's eulogy which he meets with grunts of derision. His coughing foreshadows his illness and stresses a notion of vulnerability or weakness despite his forceful glare.

▮▮▮▮▮▮▮▮▮▮▮▮▮▮▮▮▮▮▮▮▮▮▮▮▮▮▮▮▮

The post-service reception at Walt's house

Whereas his guests mingle, eat and chat, Walt is **keeping his distance**, making himself busy getting more chairs. In the basement his grandchildren find a Silver Star, which establishes Walt's past as a **Korean War Veteran**.

Walt not only treats his grandchildren with **disregard** but also for no reason **harshly fobs off** a young neighbor's (Thao) polite request for jumper cables. Stepping outside, Walt observes the neighborhood and makes a racist comment on the people who stream into his neighbor's house showing his obvious contempt for the Asians living next door.

Back inside Father Janovich approaches Walt and tells him about his late wife's wish that he should go to confession.

▮▮▮▮▮▮▮▮▮▮▮▮▮▮▮▮▮▮▮▮▮▮▮▮▮▮▮▮▮

▮▮▮▮▮▮▮▮▮▮▮▮▮▮▮▮▮▮▮▮▮▮▮▮▮▮▮▮▮

A celebration of life

When the guests are leaving, the film's focus leaves Walt and, following his gaze, moves on to the **feast at the neighbors' house** where people are celebrating a new life. Chickens are sacrificed in the backyard, a shaman blesses the newly born child, people sing and chant.

In the house, the grandmother's (Phong) words show her regret that not a man but her daughter is the **head of the household**, and that Thao, her grandson, is ordered around by his mother and sister. This is obviously against Hmong traditions which they have kept up in the US just

> *Have some goddamned respect, zipper head, we're mourning over here* (Walt to Thao)

Back on home territory Walt merely follows convention when he accepts the mourners into his house for the post-service reception. His scorn for the people around him shows in his abrasive sarcasm with which he turns down the help offered by his son or the polite request of his young neighbor. The angry, offensive silence he maintains in the presence of his grandchildren is just as inappropriate as his rude denial of the priest's offer of support. Walt is obviously not at peace with himself and thus consequently at war with the people around him. He expects the others to show respect but his own bad manners speak of nothing but arrogance and revulsion. Through the *mise-en-scène* the viewer learns about Walt's past and from this can conclude that there may be an explanation for Walt's aloofness, namely that he is dealing with experiences he does not think the young in particular can understand.

A close-up of Walt's disgusted glare across into the neighbor's yard serves as transition to the world of next door. Parallels and differences can be noted. Whereas in Walt's house people commemorate death, guests in the Vang Lor house have gathered to welcome a baby into the world. In both houses people mingle, eat and drink but the Hmong all join the shaman in the living room for a ceremony, whereas the mourners in Walt's house are depicted as single couples or small groups. Yet, in the Vang Lor house there is also someone who keeps to himself: Thao, who the viewer perceives through the frame of the kitchen door and like the **'soul calling' ceremony** in the living room proves. Thao leaves the house when he has finished the washing-up.

Two homes in perspective

The **neighboring houses** of the Kowalskis and the Vang Lors. Walt is sweeping the pavement and complaining about the **rundown state** of his neighbors' house and front yard.

recognizes as the young man so rudely sent away from Walt's doorstep. He is not included in the celebrations but is somewhat secluded and isolated in the kitchen while he is doing the dishes, a task that is not suited for a man in this culture. Then he steals away, leaving the house during the ceremony. The viewer does not know whether his fate is self-determined or imposed on him by the family.

The motif of the ambiguity belonging is thus established on the level of the characters. Two families are portrayed in which one member does not seem in the right place.

Why is he still there? (Phong about Walt)

An establishing shot of both properties brings Walt back into the picture muttering. Whereas his property is perfectly kept the Vang Lor's house is neglected. Peeling paint and a dried-up lawn make Walt groan and bemoan bygone times. In reaction to his stare, Phong, Thao's grandmother, aggressively bleats in Walt's direction. Through the funny exchange between the two cantankerous old persons, the viewer understands that the area has undergone a change: Asian immigrants have 'infiltrated' the neighborhood as Walt is one of the last original inhabitants, the others have died or moved away. Their exchange is symbolic and takes the motif to a different level. Within the urban community to which both unquestionably belong new neighbors do not speak the same language, nor do they share the same standards. Both persons perceive themselves as out of place and see the other as an intruder. Peaceful coexistence or even cooperation is unthinkable.

Father Janovich calls on Walt

The priest repeats his **offer of help** but finds the door shut in his face.

Thao and the Latino gang

Thao walking down the street, his head in a book, is provoked by members of a **Latino gang** until his cousin (Spider) with his **Hmong gang** drive up defending their territory and Thao, and request in vain that he should join them.

The problem is I think you're an overeducated, 27-year-old virgin who holds the hands of superstitious old women and promises them eternity. (Walt to Father Janovich)

In Walt's tirade the viewer can identify what motivates the embittered old man and separates him from people around, especially the priest. In Walt's world what counts is experience not education, traditional male virtues and a firm stand in the here and now. He is not willing to let people in his life (Father Janovich has to stay out on the porch, he is not welcomed in) as long as they have not yet proven themselves through their actions. Words do not matter, an education does not qualify a person to interfere in someone else's life and a man's problems can only be solved by a 'real' man. Walt's expectations are high and there are not so many people around who can live up to them.

Gran Torino. Dir. by Clint Eastwood. Actor: Bee Vang. Warner Bros Pictures 2009.

Thao and his cousin's gang

Later in front of their home Thao's sister, **Sue**, aggressively **confronts the gang** but retreats into the house before the Hmong gang leader's (Smokie) renewed attempt to **pressurize Thao into joining the gang** succeeds. Thao shows interest when Spider and Smokie ask him to steal Walt's **Gran Torino** sitting in the garage next door.

Just like at the Vang Lor house before, the mise-en-scène and the camera angle put Thao and his problem on the spot. The fence, which is shown in the film still above, serves as a border between a desolate wasteland and an average urban or suburban neighborhood and symbolizes two possible life paths. He can give into the nagging of his cousin's gang and set out on the path to delinquency or stay upright and take on the challenge of finding his place in American middle-class life.

The fact that Thao has not yet realized or at least does not confront this choice is emphasized by the way he is depicted, face down in a book, not ignorant of what is going on around him but trying hard to withdraw into his shell. Not getting into his cousin's car in the end, however, is a first indication that his instincts and his brains will hopefully guide him in the right direction.

Ride with us. (Smokie to Thao)

The scene illustrates the strategies of gang recruitment. Smokie and Spider hit *the* sore spot with Thao. He obviously feels disoriented, used and humiliated and does not know how to escape. Smokie's sturdiness and Spider's close alignment with the gang impress him. Becoming part of something seems a promising alternative even though he does not bond with his cousin emotionally. His sister's severity towards the gang is not enough for him to turn down the gang's condition for taking him on board.

Hanging out with the guys

Walt is next depicted **at a bar** drinking and cracking jokes with friends when **Father Janovich** joins them. Walt agrees to sit down and talk with him. The conversation touches on **life and death** and leaves Walt with the realization that the priest can actually relate to his experience and state of mind.

The initiation rite

When Walt sees someone shining a torch in his **garage** he arms himself and confronts the burglar, aiming the gun straight at his face. It is not clear whether he realizes that it is Thao, the Hmong boy from next door who has been forced to steal Walt's car, a 1972 Gran Torino, in a **gang initiation rite**. Walt advances on the boy until he stumbles and accidentally **fires his rifle**. The bullet hits a metal sign and Thao is able to **escape**. Spider and his gang are right behind him. Walt is on the floor coughing up blood.

By the stylistic device of contrast the viewer now observes **Walt and the guys** sharing an evening out together. The cold and grey twilight of the Lor's front yard is superseded by the dim yet cosy atmosphere of a bar. Warm lighting, Walt smiling and relaxedly telling a joke, a beer in his hands serve to convey the idea that the three men are long-time friends sharing common interests. Although the jokes are not much better and just as excluding as the gang's chunter it is clear that this is how it should be. Walt's cheerfulness and the fact that he feels comfortable show that he is bonding with these men. He seems fortified by their friendship and thus prepared to take on the young priest's insisting offer to talk. During this chat he realizes that he may know something about death because of his war experience in Korea but must admit that he is not so much able to explain what living a good life means.

Thao literally crashes into Walt's world. This scene serves as **inciting incident** for the further plot of the movie in which two worlds, represented by Walt and Thao, have now collided and become inseparable. For the viewer questions arise how Walt and Thao, so far keeping their distance through ignorance and avoidance, will clear up the mess that the gang's doings have created in their lives.

A father-son relationship

The scene abruptly changes when the viewer sees a house in a well-kept suburban part of town. In his luxuriously furnished open-space kitchen Walt's son **Mitch is talking to his father on the phone** who is attaching grids to the windows and door in his garage. Walt's suspicion that his son does not have his father's well-being in mind is confirmed when Mitch asks his dad for football tickets. Walt simply hangs up the phone.

Back to normal

Walt is seen **polishing his Gran Torino** in the driveway, then – in the evening – **smoking and having a beer** on his porch, his dog Daisy at his side. He is engrossed in his shining treasure of a car and ignores two Asian youths walking by.

Get off my lawn

At nighttime a car pulls up and **Spider and his gang** approach Thao and Sue sitting on their porch. Spider wants to take Thao by force, but **Thao refuses**. Sue tries to intervene, so does Phong. A fight breaks out, crossing the line from Thao's house and onto Walt's property. In the **commotion** two garden gnomes break and then the camera

The camera intercutting between Walt and Mitch positions the father and son in different and clearly separate environments. The dark garage in which Walt, still unsettled by the events of the night, barricades himself against the outer world is opposed to the sunlit living space in his son's house. Mitch, insouciant and selfish only shows superficial interest in his father's life. It is plain to the viewer that Walt cannot count on his son and confide in him about what is bothering him. The family does not give Walt a sense of belonging but delivers further anger and frustration on his doorstep.

The scene stresses Walt's strategy of coping with the present issues in life. The guitar chords of the theme song create a peaceful atmosphere. Aloof on his porch Walt seems sure he can literally oversee things and enjoy life. Relishing the past when things were better has nurtured a firm belief in Walt that he can find peace by keeping to himself, refusing to comprise with the inadequacies of his family and his neighborhood and thus choosing solitude over company.

This strategy of isolation consequently demands that Walt defends his territory, if necessary with armed force. With his weapon at the ready he dominates the chaos which has spread to his lawn. His warning goes out to the gang and his neighbors at the same time. Walt is protecting his property, not safeguarding his neighbors.

suddenly follows Smokie's gaze up to **Walt standing on his lawn pointing his rifle** into the gangbanger's face. The gang, obviously unnerved, retreats and drives off. Walt repeats his order to the Lor family to 'get off his lawn'.

Act Two:

In this act the protagonist must react in new surroundings and figure out the way his neighbors live their lives. This part leads to the point of no return for Walt, who will become fully committed to saving Thao even after suffering a major setback. The pace is accelerating, the conflict overwhelming: At the end of this act the protagonist is left with only one option – he must make one, last, all-or-nothing effort.

The opening scenes have presented the American suburb as two opposing settings: the world of Walt – a misanthropic, withdrawn and weakened old man, alienated from his family, critical of the church, a stranger in his neighborhood – and that of Thao and the Hmong family next door, still in touch with their cultural traditions and apart from American society, disconcerted by the American ways. Both are trapped in this hostile neighborhood which has been on a constant decline and is now controlled by gangs both sides take issue with.

The incident in Walt's garage involves the members of both worlds in a common fight against common enemies and for more mutual understanding in a changing society.

The Hero of the Neighborhood

The **motif of belonging** is taken up on a different level. Whereas act one has emphasized the differences of Walt and Thao's worlds the scenes of act two serve to demonstrate approximation and similarities. The plot focusses the viewer's attention on the true issues beyond external appearances. Motivations and beliefs will be brought out in the open and reflection on both sides sets in. The director of the movie has opted for scenes in which the characters **share** the settings which were presented in act one as belonging to one or the other. The subject of **confrontation** is slowly replaced by **encounter** and **recognition**.

Instead of a scene-to-scene approach, an assessment of how the motif is developed through scenes which are chunked helps to elicit the message the film sends.

Honouring Walt

Walt is seen at his kitchen sink. Irritated by noises outside he grabs his rifle and opens his front door. A young couple is placing a fruit platter on the steps of his porch where already more **food and flowers** are scattered. Walt is dumbfounded. He carries the flowers and food to his overflowing garbage cans and tries in vain to fend off further offerings. Between his and his neighbor's house he stops the Lor family on their way to bring Walt some plants for his garden.

He learns that **members of the Hmong community bring him gifts** to thank him for having saved Thao. Walt retorts that he only defended his property, but Sue and her mother insist that **Thao must apologize**. Walt ignores/accepts this with a further warning that should Thao ever set foot on his property again he would not show mercy.

Persisting

Father Janovich calls on Walt again who is sitting on his porch smoking. He has come because he, too, heard about what happened in the neighborhood and wants to reaffirm his hope that **a confession** would help Walt to overcome his **war trauma** and find a way to himself. Walt, impressed by the priest's persistence and verve, once again sends him away though this time rather in a disillusioned and not an aggressive tone.

Chums

Walt is **at the barber's**. The exchange of derogative remarks between him and the barber reveals their friendship and offers some orientation for how to interpret Walt's abusive language in general.

I just wanna be left alone … (Walt to the Lor family)

The first three scenes focus on Walt alone. Something has changed. Instead of his continual contemptuous side-comments Walt is actually talking, first to the Vang Lors then to the priest. Abrasive remarks are reserved for the banter with the barber and are obviously undermined by the context of their friendship.

Irritated by the presents brought to his doorstep, Walt tries to put a halt to things through appeasing gestures instead of harsh words. He listens to Sue's explanations and refutes their gratefulness with determination but is somewhat embarassed. He can even contain his anger to a certain degree when he understands that it was Thao in the garage the other night.

When Father Janovich comes to his door once again, Walt is prepared to listen and even admit that the priest has a point. Still Walt has the last word but the camera depicts the two men seeing eye to eye. Walt's stare no longer shows disdain but instead astonishment and reflection.

On the symbolic level, going for a haircut can be interpreted as the beginning of Walt's change of mind.

Back off!

In a rundown part of town **Sue** is walking with a person who is obviously her **boyfriend** (Trey), a white pretend-to-be-cool urban youth (baggy pants, a sports jersey and baseball cap worn backwards), when they are stopped by **three young black men who try to talk up Sue**. Trey tries a 'hi-five', using what he considers to be the right slang but which undoubtedly angers the black men. Sue intervenes by verbally attacking them and a tussle ensues when **Walt's pickup pulls up** and stops at a crossroads nearby. Walt observes Sue getting herself deeper into trouble as her boyfriend pulls back frightened. He drives closer and gets out of the car, first imitating then really pulling a gun from his vest to **enable Sue to climb into his car**. He then points the gun at Trey, scolding him for having sought trouble and calling the young black man 'bro' in the first place, and sends him off.

Gran Torino. Dir. by Clint Eastwood. Actor: Clint Eastwood. Warner Bros Pictures 2009.

Walt becomes part of this scene by approaching in his car, stopping and observing before acting. Again, the way he looks at what is going on tells the viewer what he is probably thinking. At first it takes a moment for him to recognize Sue among the group of youngsters, then he observes how the girl stands up to the gangbangers and realizes her defiance and courage but also her physical inferiority and the fact that she has been abandoned by her boyfriend. This is when he decides to step in. His move proves less instinctive but more thought through. The viewer can identify three stages.

Gran Torino. Dir. by Clint Eastwood. Actors (left to right): Cory Hardrict, Ahney Her, Nana Gbewonyo, Clint Eastwood. Warner Bros Pictures 2009.

A lesson in Hmong

In the car Walt reprimands Sue for playing with fire by talking to the young black men the way she did. In their conversation Sue tells Walt about **the origin and fate of the Hmong people** thus making him aware that unlike during his Korea experience these Asians were not the enemy but an American ally in the Vietnam War. Walt lets Sue know that he actually appreciates her but cannot understand her brother.

Look at that

On his porch taking up his paper Walt glances over to the Lor porch where Phong is rocking in her chair. Walt is reading out his **horoscope** to Daisy, then sees three Asian youths making fun of a white woman whose **groceries spill out on the sidewalk** when one of the bags rips. Before Walt can get up to go and help her Thao has already bent down and carries the bags to her doorstep under the watchful and acknowledging eye of Walt and Phong.

First, Walt tries with words. Only when his warning shows no effect does he feign pulling the trigger of a gun with his fingers, which surprises the gang as can be seen in the picture shown on page 41, before actually drawing a gun and pointing it both at the gangbangers for bullying Sue, and at Trey for his imitating provocation and his coward retreat.

In helping Sue in this situation Walt has crossed a line. He has stood up for someone he actually considers to be 'from the other side'. Empathizing with her distress and probably recognizing in her daring attitude the same will to persevere and not yield that he himself feels, he backs her up and takes her away in his truck.

Then how did you end up in my neighborhood? (Walt to Sue)

During their ride in Walt's truck two actually amazing things happen. For the first time in the movie Walt is asking questions and does not grunt, bellow or patronize others. He is curious and wants to know more about Sue and her culture. Sue, very articulate, cures him of his ignorance by explaining the difference between the Korean enemy and the Hmong ally. Even if he cannot forego sarcasm or lecturing the girl, his words could be that of a father. He also inquires after Thao and Sue's explanations about the boy's lack of orientation leave him thoughtful. Having taken a spontaneous liking to the young Hmong girl he also keeps an open mind towards her brother, as the viewer can see when Walt is pleasantly surprised by Thao picking up the white neighbor's groceries.

The horoscope Walt is reading foreshadows the enormous change he will face soon.

Birthday presents for Walt

Sitting at the table in his living room Walt critically eyes the **birthday cake and presents** that Mitch and his wife have brought: an old people's phone with excessively big numbers. But not enough. His son, supported by his wife, suggests that Walt **move out of his house into a retirement home**. Aggression is building up in Walt until he explodes and throws both of them out with their presents and all.

A second birthday

Back on his porch Walt admits to Daisy how much he is missing his wife. Then he sees a car pulling up to his neighbors' house and people pouring in bringing food. **Sue** approaches Walt and **invites him over**. At first reluctant, Walt agrees to go.

Inside there are a lot of people mingling, eating and talking. Walt helps himself to a beer from the fridge. Feeling ill at ease because people are not looking him into the eye he is groused by Phong. Sue deliberately mistranslates her words to a welcome. Walt receives a loud groan from all the guests when he pats a girl on the head. **Sue** feeds Walt from the barbecue roast and **explains a few cultural habits**. Later, when Sue finds Walt among the guests again he is in the middle of a staring contest with an elder man who Sue explains is the Lor family **shaman who wants to 'read' Walt.** Walt, already into his next unknown number of beer, agrees. Obviously shook up by the shaman's words Walt looks at the crowd of foreigners around him when he suddenly coughs up blood. Sue reacts but Walt dismisses her concern. Alone in the bathroom he realizes that the people in this house seem to know more about him and can **empathize more easily than his own family**.

The next scene catches Walt in the Lor kitchen where he is being served food and joking with a group of Hmong wom-

Again, two scenes are used as means of contrast. In both, human relationships are in the focus. Whereas in the first scene Walt is hurtfully humiliated by the disrespectful behavior of his son and daughter-in-law, in the second he experiences the virtues and benefits of a tightly knit community such as the Hmong families. Medium shots stress how Mitch and his wife tower over Walt and the birthday cake, how their presents misjudge his needs and how their advice is actually an infringement on his personal freedom. The buzz in the Vang Lor house tells of old and young people mingling, hosts and guests sharing a meal to which everyone has contributed and during which all seem to be enjoying each other's company.

The shaman's words, however, have utterly upset Walt. He is shocked to see that a complete stranger is able to see through him and discover his secret guilt. He feels found out but understood at the same time. Suddenly he becomes conscious of the fact that people of this foreign culture act like he believes all people should. He feels part of this community and starts seeing things and people in a different light. He begrudges having a family with whom he does not feel connected in the same way.

Walt realizes that he is now the 'exotic element' in the room and that there is a code of behavior he has to learn if he wants to participate in this community. His initiation into the community has a wobbly start but once familiarized with the customs by Sue and realizing that the foreign language does not necessarily mean a barrier he enjoys his stay and even reaches out to Thao.

Still always on the defensive and quarrelsome, Walt now allows the world of next door into his home. Women continue bringing food and flowers and Thao is finally allowed to make amends.

en. It is in these scenes in the Lor house that the viewer sees Walt smile for the first time. He follows Sue down into the **basement** where the Hmong teenagers hang about. Uncertain how to approach them he leans against a wobbly dryer which he immediately fixes. Realizing the interest one of the Hmong girls is taking in Thao, he slowly approaches Thao when the girl steps over to Walt. The rice liquor taking its toll Walt blabbers about fixing things which makes the girl laugh at him. Then she leaves followed by three suitors and **Walt** finally **addresses Thao** calling him 'toad' and reprimanding him for not taking his chance on the girl that has just left. When Walt staggers off home Thao is left confused at what just happened.

The need to make amends

Walt is mowing the lawn when two Hmong women are approaching his porch with yet more flower bouquets. At first Walt refuses but then even thanks the women for their gift. The same happens later in the day when Walt **opens his door** to other **women bringing him food**, which he accepts with obvious pleasure even letting them into his house.

When Walt pulls into his driveway he sees Sue and her mother waiting for him on the steps of his porch. A little to the side there is Thao, obviously embarrassed and insecure, hands in his pockets. Sue informs Walt that **Thao has come to make amends** and to work for Walt. Walt refuses at first, insisting that he does not want Thao on his property, but finally gives in when Sue explains that it would be an insult to their family should their offer be refused.

▷ Put the following stills in chronological order.
What has changed in the relationship between Walt and
Thao?

Gran Torino. Dir. by Clint Eastwood. Actors (left to right): Clint Eastwood, Bee Vang. Warner Bros
Pictures 2009.

Gran Torino. Dir. by Clint Eastwood. Actors (left to right): Bee Vang, Clint Eastwood. Warner Bros
Pictures 2009.

Gran Torino. Dir. by Clint Eastwood. Actors (left to right): Bee Vang, Clint Eastwood. Warner Bros Pictures 2009.

Gran Torino. Dir. by Clint Eastwood. Actors (left to right): Bee Vang, Clint Eastwood. Warner Bros Pictures 2009.

Thao's first day

Early next morning Walt, still sipping at his coffee, sees Thao sheepishly approach the Kowalski property. Towering over Thao on the lawn from his porch Walt investigates what Thao is good at. Stepping down while Thao is climbing up the stairs of the porch the two agree that **Thao should count the birds** in the tree, which the boy does.

Getting to work

When Thao comes over the following day he dares to speak out against Walt's disdainful demeanor and demands a veritable job. Looking around him, Walt decides to employ Thao for **maintenance work** on his neighbor's house. Under Walt and the neighbor's watchful eye and their incessant comments Thao sets out to work. Overlapping scenes with music in the background show **Thao slaving away in heat and rain**. Walt is meanwhile approached by more neighbors who ask for different jobs to be done by Thao.

Not a good time

Thao, callouses on his hands but with a smile on his face, walks up the stairs to Walt's porch and rings the bell. **Walt** is in the bathroom **coughing up blood**. When he opens the door to **Thao** the young man wants to know what the **chore for his last day** is and seems disappointed when Walt sends him off without one. Walt realizes this but is not able to react appropriately and shuts the door in his face.

The following scenes slowly shift the focus away from Walt to Thao and their relationship.

At first, both have to overcome their aversion and obvious distrust in the other's abilities and skills. Whereas Walt has to step down from his high horse and recognize Thao's talents and aspirations, the young man has to open up and learn to trust the gruntling old man. Quite soon he even dares to speak out and take a firm stand against Walt's bullying.

What starts out as a stopgap for the Lor's plea soon becomes a project for the reconstruction of the whole neighborhood, with Walt as the manager and Thao as the sole workforce. The young man discovers his physical strength and endurance, his obviously natural craftsmanship and also, in the exchanges with Walt, a way to speak out and defend himself with words.

Encouraged and confirmed by Sue, Walt extends his mission and becomes an even more paternal mentor for Thao when he encourages him to take on a paid job in construction so he can finance his further education. Using his contacts and paying for the necessary tools he does what a father would do for his son. Their handshake in the toolshop is symbolic. Both have grown so they can now see eye to eye.

In another world

Walt is sitting in a crowded **waiting area of a doctor's practice** when he realizes that he is **the only white person in the room**. The nurse calling him into the doctor's office seems Muslim and mispronounces his name, the doctor is Asian and tells him about a series of tests awaiting him. Walt seems confused, asking about his regular doctor who he learns retired three years ago.

The line has been cut off

Mitch and his family are in the kitchen when the phone rings. It's Walt but nobody wants to talk to him. Mitch finally picks up the call and the camera now intercuts between **Mitch and Walt** sitting on the edge of his bed with what seem to be the **test results** in front of him. After an insignificant and short exchange Mitch gets rid of Walt. When **the line is cut** there seems to be an odd intimacy between the two, Walt looking helpless and sad that he is not able to share his obviously bad news with his son, and Mitch realizing that what has not been said is actually important.

Watch it!

Walt is lighting up a cigarette on his porch while Thao is clearing out branches from their property when Spider's car slowly drives by. While Thao simply watches, Walt **points a finger gun** at Smokie. (*This kid does not have a chance.*)

But there is one thing Walt will not do. He will not confide in Thao about his serious illness. He doesn't want to burden anyone with his problems. Even though he realizes his need to share the medical results with someone he cannot bring up the courage to talk about it, neither with his son nor with Thao or Sue. So he decides to face his fate alone.

Still, sharing the space and spending time together have replaced the once hostile side by side standoff between Walt and his neighbors. The viewer perceives a natural give and take between the two households, which seems profitable to both. Whereas Walt can teach his neighbors about the 'American way of life' and provide them with practical help he can induldge in the young people's company and trust. Especially in his exchange with Sue he learns about human bonding and a way to reconcile differences he once considered irreconcilable.

Tools

Thao comes to Walt's house to inquire what he knows about faucets. In Thao's kitchen **Walt** is then **repairing the sink** and later in his garage he is taking care of the Lor's old ceiling fan with Thao watching him and inquiring about the different functions of the tools neatly stacked in the garage. When Thao regrets not being able to afford all these tools himself, Walt gives him a roll of duct tape, a pair of vise-grips and some anti-corrosion-spray for a start and **invites Thao to borrow tools** from him when needed. Thao accepts his offer gratefully. Walt coughs up blood and quickly changes the subject when Thao shows that he is worried. Instead, Thao has to explain about Spider and his gang and his botched initiation. Walt is trying to pull **an old freezer** up the stairs from the basement but does not succeed. He calls on Thao for help. When deciding who shall take the top, Thao is able to impose his will without blinking. Together they wheel the freezer to Thao's place.

A role model

Walt is sitting on his porch while Thao is polishing his Gran Torino. Sue comes along praising **Walt's positive influence on Thao**.

Plans for life

Thao is working in Walt's garden. He restates his concern for Walt, urging him to give up smoking. Again, Walt changes the subject and wants to know about **Thao's plans for**

Walt's prized possession: The 1972 Ford Gran Torino

The green two-door fastback 1972 Gran Torino Sport that Walt keeps in mint condition was a sales success for the Ford Company. Today, the **performance-oriented** model is remembered as one of the so-called 'old muscle cars' of the late sixties and early seventies. Fans go into raptures over its **no-nonsense styling**, the **sharp** fenders, the **massive** oval grille, its **muscular** shape with **angled lines** and its **potent** Cobra-Jet-engine propelling the Gran Torino from 0 to 60 mph in slightly less than 7 seconds.

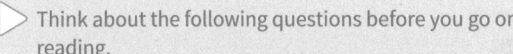

▷ Think about the following questions before you go on reading.
- How does Walt's pride in his car show?
- Do we ever see him drive the Gran Torino?
- How does Walt react when his granddaughter Ashley shows interest in the car?
- Why is Thao forgiven for his attempt to steal the Gran Torino and even inherits it in the end?

Parallels between Walt and the Gran Torino are obvious: The car serves to stress the protagonist's main characteristics. But there is more to it. Walt and Thao are connected through the Gran Torino. Representing traditionalist American values the disputed car is also a symbol of American masculinity in general. When Thao has grown into a responsible young man who holds a job in construction and has a girlfriend, he is rewarded with Walt's offer to drive his date around in the Gran Torino. Walt finally even hands the car to Thao, like a father would do to his son. And Thao shows himself worthy of it. It does not only allow for a growing mobility and freedom but also for a further acculturation into American society.

life. Thao is not sure yet, maybe sales, but he knows he lacks the money for school. **Walt encourages him to take on a job** in construction and promises to man him up a bit first.

Manning Thao up
Walt takes Thao to his friend, the barber, to learn **'how guys talk'**. When Thao imitates their ribbing word by word, they tell him off and advise him so that the second time he comes in they cannot believe their ears.

The right words
Walt has vouched for Thao at a construction site. In the talk with the job supervisor, Thao does everything right, looks the man into the eye and finds the right words. **Thao gets the job**.

Proper tools
In town **Walt buys Thao a tool belt, utility knife holder and hardware holder** promising to lend him the tools from his garage. Thao shows his appreciation and they **shake hands**.

"This is the way guys talk"

The screenwriter Nick Schenk fills Walt's dialogue with racist language. These scenes, especially the one where Walt takes Thao to his friend the barber to teach him how to *talk like a man*, come across as funny and astute. Looking closer at the use of labels in *Gran Torino* one can see that different issues come into focus. When Walt talks about or to Hmong people, he comes across as insulting and hateful. But when he is using insulting labels with his friends at the barber shop or the bar, these labels actually seem to communicate his affection for his friends. Critics have observed, however, that some people in the audience not only just laugh but seem to be laughing in agreement. This would make the use of racial slurs questionable in a film that stands up against prejudice and racism.

 Take a look at some of the slurs used by Walt in the film. Put them into context by looking at the respective scenes they are taken from to see…
- whom Walt addresses.
- in which tone these slurs are uttered.
- what the underlying message is.

A Pollack and a Chink (Martin, the barber). *Gook. You dumb, Italian-Wop-Dago. Zipperhead. And you should ask out Yum Yum too. Dragon lady. Toad. Son of a bitch. Egg roll. Swamp rats. Hell, even Toad isn't driving me nuts for once. Slope. Goofball. If you live that long, dipshit. I'll send you a fucking fruitcake at Christmas.*

The analysis shows that in the movie the context decides whether a label or an expression is meant as a **demeaning** and **disrespectful** (e. g. *How many swamp rats can you get into one room?*), or an **insulting** (e. g. *And have some goddamned respect, zipperhead, we're mourning*

What now?

Thao gets off the bus, safety helmet under his arm. Jogging lightly through some back alleys he is confronted by Spider and his gang pulling up in their Honda. He remains calm, but **the gangbangers take Thao's tools off him** and destroy them. Smokie stubs out a cigarette on Thao's face. Thao screams.

It is not your problem

Walt is taking out his trash when he spots Thao in the back alley. He wrings the truth out of the boy and **offers his help** but Thao simply refuses to accept a new tool.

Lay your hands off him

Walt **attacks Smokie** outside of his home and demands that the gang leaves Thao alone or suffer the consequences. Walt returns home in the rain.

Why not the Gran Torino?

Walt is having Thao, his sister and mother and Wa Xam (Youa) over for a barbecue in his backyard. They joke and laugh together. **Walt offers Thao his Gran Torino** for a night out with his new girlfriend. Thao cannot believe his luck and Walt seems surprised by his own generosity and trust.

over here.), or an **affectionate** (e.g. *You dumb, Italian-Wop-Dago*) utterance. The viewer can also observe that there is a change in Walt's use of labels parallel to a change in his attitude towards his neighbors. However, use of racial slurs does not subside throughout the film.

▷ Form your own opinion on the question whether screenwriter and director should have been more careful about the use of language in Gran Torino. Therefore, find a partner to discuss the following statements.

- Walt and Martin trading insults is funny.
- Name-calling when talking about others, and not with them, is no problem.
- Swearing and using strong language is not appropriate for a Hollywood film.
- Racial slurs – even if used affectionately – are never okay.
- If people have a penchant for using slurs, they are xenophobic and racist.

It's not your problem. (Thao to Walt)

Thao has grown into a mature and self-confident young man who is ready to take responsibility for himself and is on the way to find his place in life. When Walt entrusts his Gran Torino to Thao and Wa Xam (Youa) for their first night out, it seems as if a happy ending is near.

Even the gang's attack, although a setback for his self-assurance at first, cannot stop Thao from determinedly continuing his way. So he turns down Walt's offer to help in buying new tools and does not want him to confront the gang. The fact that he – just like Walt before – does not want to burden their friendship with what he considers 'his' problems proves that they find themselves on equal terms.

No, no, no

Walt is watching baseball at night when Spider drives up at the Lor's house. From their car **the gang opens fire and shoots up Thao's house** before disappearing back into the night. Walt runs over to find the Lor family in great confusion but unhurt, except for Thao. Thao has suffered a slight cut on his neck. Sue has gone out to her aunt's.

Walt is waiting up with Thao, his mother and grandmother. Suddenly Phong runs to open the door for **Sue who walks in battered and bruised**. Her clothes are torn, blood is running down between her legs, everybody moans and screams. Walt is in shock, Phong points at him screeching. He leaves constantly muttering 'no'.

Back at his house he demolishes his kitchen, finally sinking into his chair completely exhausted and breathing heavily. When the camera moves up from his hands there are tears running down his face.

Act Three:

The protagonist determines his own fate, Walt is facing his hardest challenge which takes him and the plot to the ultimate show down. Thao is saved despite himself and the movie ends on a conciliatory note even if Walt has seen no other way than to sacrifice his life so that the actual culprits can finally be handed over to justice and the neighborhood be made a better place.

But it is Walt who cannot let go and passes up on the opportunity of breaking the cycle of violence that prevents true change from happening in the neighborhood. It is as if he were acting on trained impulse. He has let Thao into his world, he feels responsible for him now and so he doggedly follows the principle of 'an eye for an eye', miscalculating the consequences of his violent assault on Smokie.

The outcome is fatal. Not only does the gang take it out on Sue, her mother and grandmother, scaring them for life but it also throws Thao off his course. Walt understands this but it is too late.

Redemption

The final act examines the thin line between acting out for others and self-sacrifice. The **theme of belonging** reinforces this examination because even if Walt finally knows where he belongs the liberation and content-ment this brings is short-lived. By bonding with Thao and his family, Walt has also embraced their problems because he quickly realizes that their exclusion from mainstream society and the violence of the gang in

Nothing is fair

A little later but still at night, **Father Janovich** lets himself in. They talk quietly over a can of beer. The priest, disillusioned and lost for words for once, wants to know about **Walt's plans** should Thao confront him with plans for revenge. Walt has no answer yet.

This is going to end

The next morning Thao barges into Walt's kitchen calling for action. Walt pleads with him to stay calm but **Thao is too worked up** to listen. Walt makes him sit down to work out a plan. Reluctantly Thao agrees to come back at four p.m. to learn about the plan Walt will think out for them.

particular threaten not only their well-being alone. When failed by the government, all people in the neglected neighborhoods of modern suburban America face the same fate and have to look after themselves with the means they have. Mutual care and solidarity are a necessity in this fight against hopelessness, deterioration and crime. This is what Walt comprehends once he has accepted that the world he knew no longer exists. To find peace and contentment he opened up and traded his prejudice for understanding. He has gained love and respect in return for his effort and can feel like part of something greater.

So it is the feeling of belonging that inspires in Walt the courage to provide Thao and Sue a safer future and at the same time finally face and redeem his own past.

In the first two scenes of the final act Walt is once more in the spotlight. The light atmosphere of the days before Sue's rape has gone. Walt is back in the shadows of his house alone, yet this time visitors are welcome. Brooding over how he can make up for his mistake he asks the priest about what he would do. Although the priest warns him not to drag Thao further into the mess he evades Walt's question and hopes that talking may stop the old man from taking revenge. But Walt is determined that he cannot simply ignore the situation and that his affiliation with the Hmong community demands one final effort of him, though definitely not of Thao whom he wants to keep safe.

Preparations

Walt is **following routines**: he mows his lawn, later soaks in the bathtub, has his hair cut at the barber's (Martin), is fitted for a new suit and goes to Father Janovich's church for **confession**. He confesses to having kissed another woman, a ridiculous tax fraud, and not having been close enough to his two sons. The **priest pleads with him** not to seek revenge but Walt does not react.

Back in his house Walt is **cleaning his weapons** when **Thao** walks in and immediately picks up the rifle. Walt takes him to the basement, telling him about how he received the **Silver Star** in Korea and now pinning it onto Thao's chest to observe his courage. Thao wants to know how many men Walt killed in Korea and what it felt like. Walt confesses to 13 or more but evades the second answer, asking Thao to close up the chest. Thao must then realize that Walt has fooled him by **locking him up** in the basement. Through the metal mash of the basement door, which reminds the viewer of the confessional box in church, Walt delivers his true confession to Thao about how he killed a young and scared Korean kid with the rifle, even though the child was willing to surrender, and how this **killing has haunted him** until today, even more so because he received a medal for this. Since he already has got blood on his hands and is thus soiled he will go alone, sparing Thao a similar fate. **Thao revolts** in vain.

Walt says goodbye to Daisy and leaves her on the neighbor's porch with Phong.

Gran Torino. Dir. by Clint Eastwood. Actor: Clint Eastwood. Warner Bros Pictures 2009.

Walt has decided on how to act but he will not let anybody know. Although he obviously wants to leave the stage with all things necessary sorted out, his family do not play a part in his farewell to the world, not even in his will.

Walt has even made up his mind to confess. He allows the priest and God to deal with his minor misdemeanors but keeps his irredeemable sin to himself until he sees how Thao is filled with the same vindictiveness he once felt.

Knowing what evil this can do he completes his confession in front of Thao, teaching him a final lesson. The resolution and remedy of what led to Sue's rape does not lie in retribution but in the uncompromising determination to do what is right and continue down the good way. Every individual must contribute to make the world a better place.

Redemption lies in forgiveness but Walt cannot forgive himself and can thus only redeem his sin by giving away his own life for the good cause. In only provoking the gangsters he does not burden himself with more guilt but has the authorities do their job.

Finishing things

Sue is woken up by her mobile ringing. It is Walt who informs her about how to let her brother out of his basement. Before she can say anything he hangs up. Ignoring Phong's screeching she runs over to Walt's house.

Father Janovich is talking to two police officers **in front of Smokie's home**. He wants them to stay but **the authorities** refuse to become involved and the priest leaves with them.

Sue frees **Thao** who informs her that Walt is on his way to Smokie's. They both run out of the house.

Walt can be seen outside of Smokie's house from which loud voices can be heard. Through the blinds they perceive **Walt's shadow** and come out. Walt immediately starts insulting them. In reaction Spider points a gun at Walt. Neighbors can be seen peering out from behind their doors and windows. Walt's hand goes to his pocket and takes out a cigarette, immediately more guns are pointed in his direction. **Walt points finger guns** at the gangbangers. When he slowly puts his hand into the inner pocket of his vest and quickly draws it out again, the **gangbangers** simultaneously level their guns and **fire**. Walt's body is riddled with bullets – he falls backwards onto the sidewalk, landing on his back, arms outstretched, lighter in his right hand.

The theme of Gran Torino sets in. Sue and Thao arrive at the scene when the police are already there, lights flickering through the night. One of the officers informs them that **Walt was unarmed** and the gang will be put behind bars for a long time. They and Father Janovich watch as Walt's body is lifted into the ambulance and the gangbangers are **taken away by the police**. The scene fades out on the Silver Star still dangling from Thao's breast.

He dies in peace, leaving Thao his Silver Star and his Gran Torino, both essentially American and symbols of what needs to be reconciled in American society. Thao knows that the old man believed enough in his integrity and strength to entrust him with his legacy: to help create a world in which there is less room for destructive prejudice and harmful hatred but the possibility to acknowledge the other and create a sense of belonging for everyone who has made his home in the US.

▐█▌█▐█▌█▐█▌█▐█▌█▐█▌█▐█▌█▐█▌█▐█▌█▐█▌█▐█▌█▐█▌█▐█▌█▐█▌█▐█▌

Another funeral service

In traditional Hmong dress Sue and Thao leave for Walt's funeral with their mother. Phong stays behind on the porch with Daisy.

It seems like the same church as in the beginning and people are entering. Walt, dressed in his new suit, lies in an open coffin, his sons with their family and Sue and Thao sit in the front rows. Today the **atmosphere is tense and sad**. Nobody dares talking. Father Janovich steps up and begins his eulogy with the **anecdote** of how Walt had once told him that such a young ignorant man could not know anything about life or death.

To my friend

The family and Sue and Thao are gathered **in a law office** where a lawyer reads out **Walt's last will** in which he leaves his house to the church because his wife would have liked that. Furthermore, he **leaves his 1972 Gran Torino** to his friend Thao. The scene fades from Thao's smiling face to him driving the Gran Torino with Daisy at his side along Lake Michigan. Walt is singing the theme song.

▐█▌█▐█▌█▐█▌█▐█▌█▐█▌█▐█▌█▐█▌█▐█▌█▐█▌█▐█▌█▐█▌█▐█▌█▐█▌█▐█▌

Some quotes

▷ Read the given quotes and match them to a passage of the analysis so that they exemplify or illustrate the point made.

1 Walt: I lived with death for three years in Korea. We shot people, we stabbed them with bayonets, we hacked seventeen-year-old kids to death with shovels, for Christ's sake. I did things that won't leave me till the day I die, horrible things, things I have to live with.
Father Janovich: And what about life?
Walt: Well … I survived the war … got married … and raised a family.
Father Janovich: Sounds like you know more about death than you do about living.
Walt: Maybe so.

2 Sue: The girls go to college, the boys go to jail.

3 Horoscope: Your birthday today; This year you have to make a choice between two life paths. Second chances come your way. Extraordinary events culminate in what might seem to be an anti-climax. Your lucks numbers are: 84, 23,11, 78 and 99.

4 Kor Khue/Sue: He says people do not respect you. They do not even want to look at you. He says the way you live your food has no flavor. You're worried about your life. You made a mistake in your past life like a mistake you did you are not satisfied with. He says you have no happiness in your life. It's like you're not at peace.

5 Walt: I got blood on my hands. I'm soiled. This is why I'm going alone tonight.

6 Thao: Go ahead. I don't care if you insult me or say racist things 'cause you know what I'll take it.

Other central themes in *Gran Torino*

The movie *Gran Torino* contains a roller coaster of events and surprising twists in relationships, funny moments and serious drama. Its ending is tragic but at the same time comforting, providing hope for better times ahead. A multitude of themes set the plot in motion which address contemporary issues and questions the meaning of life.
Let us have a closer look at some of these.

Overcoming prejudice in US American culturally interlaced society

The action of *Gran Torino* is set in a **formerly white, working-class suburb** in the Detroit area of Michigan, today populated only by very few remaining blue-collar workers and their families and dominated by **poor Asian immigrants**. The neighborhood's houses and properties are **in decay**, **xenophobia and ethnic segregation** keep their inhabitants apart, gang violence is commonplace. **Societal norms are shifting** and need redefining. Walt Kowalski and the Vang Lor family are members of two **vastly different cultures**, initially **separated by fear** of each other and prejudice against one another. It is not only the **language** which separates the neighbors. The barriers that divide them find expression in the **customs** of Walt's neighbors, which come across as exotic and uncivilized to a rather conventional American like him. Moreover, Walt is an aging veteran whose bitter memories of **the Korean War** have left him with a deeply ingrained bias against everything Asian. He thus sees his **former enemy** not only in the violent Asian gangs but also in his upright Hmong neighbors who actually suffer just the same from the economic decline of the area and the continual disturbances in the once quiet neighborhood. When the neighboring family insists that their teenage son, Thao, make amends for trying to steal Walt's car the grumbling old man is drawn into a world which he learns resembles his own more than he could have ever imagined. **Accepting obvious differences, overcoming hurtful prejudices** and **adapting to a necessary change** call for an open mind, which Walt shows he has. He first connects with Thao's older sister because he can easily relate to her quick-wittedness, her courage and her fighting spirit, qualities he respects. Through her he learns that despite all the weird outlooks of this family's traditions they **share the same moral code**: success in life comes only through **hard and honest work**, family stands for **mutual care and support** in any situation, and a person's value is measured by the effectiveness of their actions. Realizing that his own family falls short of these requirements Walt turns to his neighbors and does everything in his power to safeguard Thao's future. Through coming to terms with the past and opening up to a new world Walt is rewarded with **respect** and **friendship**. "Me versus them" is replaced by **"united we stand"** and Thao carries this hopeful lesson into the future.

Recognizing the other and realizing **common values** shared in both communities surmount cultural differences and become the tools that help people to connect and create a **peaceful coexistence of various cultures**. These tools enable people of different ethnic backgrounds to work and live together. The movie *Gran Torino* shows how communicating and uniting despite all differences means peace and a better life for all.

Defining masculinity and heroism

Movies in general and Hollywood blockbusters in particular tend to portray male behavior in idealized, heroic terms, where boys and young men learn how to make things right, stand up for themselves, stay firm against injustice and, in the end, make a sacrifice for the greater good, often with fists or a gun. Through their power of suggestion movies define the **American hero** as **male, outgoing, strong and active**. In *Gran Torino*, too, the hero is male, stands tall and fights for the greater good.

Masculinity

Walt Kowalski is a highly decorated war veteran. Resisting the gang by **force of arms** he becomes a hero among the Hmong community and by **sacrificing his life** he dies in battle for the good cause. He is **taciturn, physically strong, and mentally tough**. **Self-reliant** and **determined** he believes in hard work and the 2nd Amendment. Walt, the main character of the movie *Gran Torino*, has all the common qualities of a hero. Thao, on the other hand, needs *manning up*. At home his mother, grandmother and sister bemoan his feminine touch while voluntarily accepting his help in the household. Walt consequently sees him as a sissy, mocks his impassiveness and bosses him around until he notices him 'doing the right thing' by helping a neighbor with her groceries. Walt takes Thao under his wing and teaches him all a man needs to know – how to **handle tools**, **polish the car**, and **impress the girls**. **Self-respect** and **self-reliance**, **determination** and **persistence**, and the pursuit of **a strict moral code** is also important. Yet, these concepts of masculinity and heroism are also questioned in the film. The male hero is ageing, he is weakened through illness and his course of action, although successful, leads to his own death. During the movie Walt and the viewer realize that a **different approach** and **different tools** are needed to **meet the challenges of a modern world** going through continual change. So Walt makes way for a future generation in which masculinity and heroism are newly defined.

Heroism

Walt has grown up to see the world in black and white, dividing it into 'us' and 'them', and he has learned to **confront**, **combat** or **dominate** everything and everyone who seemingly **threatens his world through their otherness**. In Korea he protected his country, in the suburb he now protects his lawn. The enemy is different and yet the same. In the 1950s, US troops, with men like Walt Kowalski, were sent to southeast Asia when the US supported UN forces protecting South Korea against the forces of North Korea, who were supported by their ally, the Soviet Union. In a relatively short but exceptionally bloody war more than 5 million soldiers and civilians lost their lives in a military conflict that became a symbol of the global struggle between East and West. **Good and evil** were clearly defined for US American soldiers, whose struggles and sufferings unlike in WWII did not receive very much attention or appreciation back home, because of only little media coverage. In the name of the US the soldiers were **fighting to liberate the world** by defeating evil communism. The fighting was fierce and traumatizing. In the beginning, the young men who were rushed to the front line were often undertrained and underprepared. Later, US soldiers recalled that they were sometimes ordered to shoot on sight, no matter whether it meant killing enemy soldiers, refugees or civilians. After the war was over, inexplicable anxieties, upsetting memories in flashbacks, bad dreams and nightmares, and continuing difficulties in controlling emotions or sudden aggression came back to haunt the men for the rest of their lives. It is obvious that Walt did not escape this war undamaged either. In particular, his raging need to defend himself and his territory are obvious throughout the film. In ignorance he confuses the Hmong next door with the Koreans of his past – all Asians seem to fit his learned concept of the enemy and represent a threat to him and his world. In defense of what is his, he falls back on the force of arms, his old army rifle which symbolizes dominance and guarantees the wanted outcome of any conflict. Just like in his military career he is not prepared to rely on others such as the police or mediators to handle conflicts in his civilian life. And just like back then, opening up and sharing his state of mind with anybody is also out of the question. The local priest does not stand a chance, as Walt will not confide in him or anyone else but continues to **struggle and overcome the trauma and guilt all by himself**. Walt is stuck in his ways, the old ways, so he cannot change even after he has learned to differentiate between past and present, between the harmless Hmong community and the Korean enemy or Asian gang, between friend and foe. Although he has now included Thao and his family in what he is firmly resolved to protect, his weapon of choice literally stays the same.

In Thao, however, Walt has successfully implanted a different kind of weapon. He has 'manned Thao up', not by training this introverted kid in the use of firearms but by building up his **self-confidence**, giving him lessons on **self-esteem**, **audacity** and **responsibility**, developing the skills this young man had not yet discovered in himself, and teaching him how to communicate with confidence to obtain his goals. Thao's **composure**, his **ability to endure and reflect**, his **keen eye**, his **sensitivity and obvious empathy** seem like the effective transformation of qualities laid out but repressed in Walt. When Thao drives off in the sunset the viewer believes that with him the world has changed for the better.

The meaning of life and death

When the local priest corners Walt in the bar he wants to talk about 'life and death'. Walt mocks the young man for his **inexperience**, only to realize that the priest may have something to say about death but not that much about life. The verbal exchange between the two characters offers a motif that occurs and reoccurs throughout the film and becomes one of its central themes: life and death, and how the two are **inextricably connected**. Throughout his life, Walt Kowalski has encountered death in various forms: as a soldier he killed and saw comrades be killed in Korea, his wife has recently passed away and her death leaves him lonely and sad, gang violence in his neighborhood is claiming victims on a daily basis and continually revives his memories of war and hate. Now he is faced with his own death when he learns that he is suffering from lung cancer. To Walt, **death is barbaric and outrageous**, an experience that has alienated him from others since he refuses to let other people share in his grievance. Calm and dispassionate he perceives his own **death as inevitable though controllable** in the sense that he is determined to decide the how, the when, and above all the what to die for. In his **self-sacrifice** he seeks both **retaliation** for what the gang has done to Thao and his sister and **redemption** for his own sins.

As you have probably noticed by working through the scene-by-scene analysis above (pp. 18 ff.), it takes more than one sentence to explain what the essence of the movie is about.

Rounding off

▷ Now reconsider the plot summary of page 15 and the one beneath to decide which one you prefer.

Walt Kowalski, a retired auto worker, recently widowed and alienated from his sons and their families, fills his days with home repair, a beer on the porch and a monthly trip to his only friend, the barber. With suspicion he observes the changes in his neighborhood. As a Korean War veteran he cultivates his prejudice against anything Asian and sees his peace being increasingly disturbed by the Hmong immigrants who have replaced his former neighbors. One night when someone tries to steal his prized Gran Torino, Walt involuntarily becomes involved in the problems of the family next door and finds himself mentoring the shy teenaged Thao to stand up against gang pressure and find direction in life. The unlikely friendship that develops will change both their lives dramatically and replace ignorance and prejudice through understanding and mutual respect.

▷ And now it is up to you to put your observations into words. The following vocab box may help you.

Vocab: Central themes

a bitter/cantankerous man – set in his ways – hassled by – an overzealous priest – ungrateful and condescending children – spoiled grandkids – fed up/resentful of the changing face of the neighborhood – once populated by white, working-class people – become a haven for Asian immigrants – irritated by rites and traditions of his next-door Asian neighbors – grumble – gangs controlling the neighborhood – repeatedly try to recruit – shy/bashful/introverted/impassive boy – keep to himself – gang-banging cousins – rough sb. up/give sb. a hard time – point a shotgun at – scare sb. away – shower the porch with – show one's gratitude for – persuade sb. to – a prized possession – be caught off-guard by – threaten sb. at gunpoint – as atonement/to make amends – give sb. a tedious task – fix up a house – regard sb. with disdain – learn about – warm up to – harass/bother sb. – act as a mentor for sb. – find guidance in sb. – lecture sb. on sth. – get a job in construction – be mugged by – become enraged – threaten sb. with death – lead to more retaliation from – put off sb. – outwit sb. – discuss sth. with sb. – oppose/approve of violence – seek revenge on – head to – out on the front porch – a standoff – pull weapons – assume sth. – shoot sb. down – be completely unarmed – entrust sth. to – the final scene features

Character breakdowns

Now that you have analysed the film in detail, the insight you have gained can help you create profiles for the characters involved.

On page 82/83 there is a chart to begin with.

1▷ First consider the logic behind the chart. What do the bold print and the font size suggest?

2▷ Use the chart and the vocab below to explain how the characters correlate during the movie. Draw arrows and label them.

Vocab: Relationships

How people relate to one another	
Problemfamilie; gestörte Beziehungen innerhalb der Familie	dysfunctional family
enge Familienbande	a close-knit family
sich um jdn. kümmern	to look after sb./to take care of sb.
eine Beziehung zu jdm. finden	to relate to sb.
sich einmischen	to interfere
in einer Situation schlichten, helfend eingreifen	to intervene
ein langjähriger Freund	a long-time friend
mit jdm. ausgehen	to date sb.
jdm. entgegentreten; jdn. mit etwas konfrontieren	to confront sb. (with sth.)
mit jdm. auskommen	to get along with sb.
jdm. aus dem Weg gehen	to avoid sb.
etwas wieder gutmachen	to make amends
jdm. eine Standpauke halten	to lecture sb.

jdm. Vorwürfe machen	to reproach sb.
jdn. enttäuschen	to disappoint sb.
jdn. demütigen	to humiliate sb.
jdn. angreifen	to attack sb. verbally, physically
sich von jdm. abwenden	to turn one's back to
jdn. für etwas verantwortlich machen	to hold sb. accountable for sth.
sich opfern für	to sacrifice oneself for

What strong relationships are built on		What harms relationships	
affection	loyalty	disregard	disdain
trust	empathy/ considera- tion	ignorance	aversion
kindness	generosity	selfishness	greed
tolerance	respect	prejudice/ bias	neglect
confidence	patience	distrust	jealousy/ envy

Character map

Martin
Walt's barber and friend

Tim Kennedy
Walt's acquaintance, a construction
coordinator

WALT KOWALSKI

Father Janovich
Catholic priest in the parish
working with the neighborhood

Steve Kowalski
Walt's younger son

Mitch and Karen Kowalski
Walt's older son and wife

Josh and Ashley Kowalski
Walt's grandchildren
(Mitch and Karen's cildren)

Kor Khue
the Lor Family shaman

Vu
Thao's timid mother

Phong
Thao's cantankerous grandmother

THAO VANG LOR

Youa (Wa Xam)
Thao's girlfriend

Black Gang

Latino Gang

Sue Lor
Thao's streetwise sister

Spider
Thao's cousin
and Smokie
Hmong Gang

Trey
Sue's one-time date

Character outlines

Before studying the given outlines of the main characters let us consider how we form a first impression about people in general.

1▷ Review scenes in which you have a particularly vivid memory of a character.
Discuss some of the following criteria with a partner to gain a deeper insight into the characters.

1 What does the name tell about the person? (ethnic origin, nickname, shortened form)

2 Does the character have any distinguishing features (tattoos, scars, birthmarks)?

3 What is the character's preferred outfit?

4 What accessories are associated with the character?

5 What is his/her usual level of grooming? (unobtrusive, disheveled, smart, very put together, untidy but clean, etc.)

6 Does the character have any distinguishing 'tics' or mannerisms?

7 Does the way he/she walks betray his/her level of self-confidence? (confident, powerful strides, lazy stroll, fast, bent, walks at a clip, distracted, eyes on the ground)

8 How does the character talk (rapid, slow, measured, drawl, etc.)?

9 What is the style of his/her speech (elevated, educated, peppered with slang, etc.)?

10 What about his/her posture (stiff, military, slouching, casual and relaxed, turtle, tired)?

11 Does the character gesture? (only when agitated or eager, not at all, compulsive 'hand-talker', controlled, only to make a point)

12 How much eye contact does the character like to make (direct, shifty, etc.)?

13 What is the character's catchphrase and/or preferred curse word?

14 Does the character wear his/her emotions on their sleeve?

2> How do all these aspects influence the viewer's opinion of the character?

The two protagonists …

 Look at the expressions in the box beneath and match them to either Walt or Thao. Think of scenes that illustrate the various aspects of their personality.

embittered	disoriented and stuck
brainy and smart	estranged from his family
torn	resigned
astute and quick on the uptake	good-natured

 Highlight key words and expressions (adjectives).

grew

Walt (pp. 86, 88, 90)

As the son of Polish immigrants **Walt** grew up in Detroit, Michigan and has spent his whole life there, except for the time he served in the United States military during the Korean War. The intense, life-changing moment when he killed a young Korean on the run has haunted him ever since. His traumatic experience has shaped his bitter personality and he has retained a deep dislike of Asian people. Wartime camaraderie has also shaped his language and his inclination towards racist banter and cynic evasion of serious exchange.

Back from the war he started working at a Ford automobile plant and helped build the 1972 Gran Torino, which has been his pride and joy ever since. He married, moved to the suburbs and had two sons. His conservative family values and respect for honesty, hard work, and self-reliance are defined by the blue-collar ethics of the 1950s when America took pride in the physical strength and manual skills of men in the workforce.

Walt's wife has recently died and he now finds himself alone in the house.

Now use the expressions to create their character portrait. Compare your texts to the profiles beneath.

ready to use armed force	impassive
impetuous	willing to learn
ready to self-sacrifice	squinting and growling
fierce and uncompromising	withdrawn

up

Thao (pp. 87, 89, 91)

The Hmong adolescent boy has grown up as the only male member of the household. His family, consisting of a quarrelsome grandmother, a shy mother but a very persistent older sister, came as refugees from the hills of Laos to the US in the 1970s. Once settled, the Hmong have only partly assimilated and rather continue to live their culture in close-knit communities, mostly in the northeast of the US. The large Hmong community in Highland Park, Michigan has taken over the houses in which former workers like Walt lived. The older generation, like Thao's grandmother and his mother, do not speak English and continue to raise their children in the traditions of their people. This is why young people like Thao live in-between two worlds.

Thao has successfully finished high school, just like his sister he is fluent in English and open to the American way of life but not yet acquainted enough.

now

With indignation **Walt** observes how the 'old neighborhood' he has lived in all his life has been taken over by Asian immigrants who do not speak his language and let the once well-kept properties fall into disrepair. Walt in contrast meticulously tends to his house and car. Alienated from his ungrateful and greedy sons and not very sociable as such he prefers to pass his days alone, his dog Daisy at his side. Only sometimes does he go and see his friend the barber or share a beer and a joke with friends from back then at the local bar. He seems to have lost faith and so he turns down the local priest's offer to help him unload his guilt.

meeting the

Over the years, **Walt** has turned into a grumpy, tough-minded, unhappy old man who does not allow anyone to get close. In particular the Asians in his neighborhood and the young priest are in focus when he puts his frustration into words. With his derogative language, his racist remarks and coarse manners he offends and humiliates them in the hope they will disappear into thin air. But on the contrary: against his will Walt becomes drawn into the life of his Hmong neighbors. First, he finds the boy from next door trying to steal the Gran Torino from his garage and next he has to defend his property against their cousin's gang. Through this act he unintentionally becomes this family's hero and to his surprise finds himself in charge of educating young Thao.

With Sue as a clever mediator Walt has to break with his prejudice and discovers a foreign culture in which he can feel at home. And more, the young people from next door quickly grow on him because they see though his façade and offer him their trust and friendship. And he enjoys hav-

living

As an introvert who enjoys reading and rather keeps to himself **Thao** constantly earns scorn from all sides. His grandmother mocks him because under his mother and sister's thumb he gullibly takes on all the household tasks they dump on him. Impassive and evasive he does not show any particular interest or skills nor does he take any initiative towards his future. Not having known a male role model he is disoriented and lacks the inner strength and resilience to find his way himself.

challenge

Insecure and helplessly exposed to the bullying of the various gangs in the neighborhood **Thao** desperately searches for direction. His cousin Spider talks him into seeking the protection of the gang to gain self-confidence and become a man. Thao is unconvinced but submits. For his initiation he has to steal from his neighbor. His tentative attempt fails and like his family he is intent on making amends to Walt, who has been befriended by his sister Sue.

At first irritated by Walt's cynicism he stoically slaves for the neighborhood for two weeks and finally earns respect from Walt, and more. His new mentor initiates Thao in the prospects of a rewarding adult life, possible university studies, a girlfriend, and a job. Walt invests in him, buying him the necessary tools and teaching him their use. Thao admires Walt's self-confidence, his courage and intransigence when it comes to defending right against wrong.

So, when his sister is violently assaulted Thao, protective of his family, wants to seek revenge and relies on Walt to show

ing something to teach Thao – his manual skills, the male self-confidence he represents and his understanding of the American way of life guide the young man so he can take life into his own hands. Like a father, Walt's urge to protect Thao and Sue from harm makes him take up the fight against the gang violence in the neighborhood. He, however, underestimate the cycle of violence to which he contributes and which will demand his self-sacrifice in the end. To secure Thao and Sue's future he willingly gives his life thereby hoping to also redeem the sin of his past. He dies at peace with himself.

him the way. But his mentor will not let him because he has decided to carry the burden alone. In this last lesson Walt teaches him, Thao learns that the cycle of violence needs to be broken and that by walking away instead of contributing to the violence he can secure a future not only for himself, but also for his family.

... and their mediators

Sue

Thao's sister seems more agile and streetwise than her brother. Relentlessly, she pushes her cousin and his gang away to protect Thao from following the fate of so many young Hmong. Also, she courageously confronts the black gangbangers. Knowing that she is physically inferior she fights with words. Her strong and independent spirit enable her to move easily between the worlds of the Hmong and the American suburb. She senses Walt's false perceptions and knows exactly how to explain her world to him. With a lot of persistence she convinces Walt to look after her brother and enjoys the way the two relate. Her commitment to her brother and her trust in Walt, however, do not pay off for her. She becomes the innocent victim in the cycle of violence that holds the neighborhood captive and to which Walt contributes once too often.

Father Janovich

The good-natured priest promised Walt's wife that he would convince her troubled husband to make a confession. He takes his promise seriously and repeatedly pays visits to Walt, who keeps rejecting his help with mockery and insults. Calling the priest an *inexperienced, over-educated, 27-year-old virgin* Walt makes clear that he does not take the young man seriously when he insists on discussing questions of *life and death* with him. Janovich's sensitivity, persistence and passion, however, finally enable him to get through to Walt and understand the man and his motives better. Walt, too, must recognize that the young priest has a point and confides in him when he says that he is *most haunted by what he was not ordered to do*. Although unevenly matched the two men open up to each other and learn from each other.

A final evaluation

The lyrics of the **theme song** allude to various scenes of the film and illustrate once more the theme of identity and the motif of **the ambiguity of belonging**.

 Match the aspects of the analysis given on the following page to lines from the song on this page.

1. So tenderly
2. your story is nothing more than what you see
3. or what you've done or will become
4. Standing strong
5. do you belong in your skin
6. Just wondering
7. Gentle now
8. the tender breeze blows whispers through
9. my Gran Torino
10. Whistling another tired song
11. Engine hums
12. and bitter dreams grow, heart locked
13. in a Gran Torino
14. It beats a lonely rhythm all night long […]
15. Realign all the stars above my head
16. Warning signs travel far
17. I drink instead on my own
18. Oh, how I've known the battle scars and worn out beds […]
19. These streets are old
20. they shine with the things I've known
21. and breaks through the trees, their sparkling
22. Your world is nothing more
23. than all the tiny things you've left behind […]
24. May I be so bold and stay
25. I need someone to hold
26. that shudders my skin, their sparkling […]

Text, (OT): Cullum, James / Eastwood, Clint / Eastwood, Kyle / Stevens, Michael Christopher

Copyright: Cibie Music / EMI Music Publishing Ltd / Robie Springs Music / Upward and onward / Wallet Music / Warner Olive Music LLC / Warner-Barham Music LLC Neue Welt Musikverlag GmbH, Hamburg / EMI Music Publishing Germany GmbH, Berlin / Universal Music Publishing GmbH, Berlin

a) all people need someone to hold onto

b) everybody gets to write their own life story

c) everything changes in life except for what you do not allow to change

d) human life is fragile

e) life is collected experience

f) living their lives people lose their innocence

g) man is shaped by experience

h) people must learn to stand up for themselves and take responsibility for their lives

i) there are always regrets in looking back

j) there are constant reminders of dreams that have become compromised

k) there is always hope for the better

Solutions

About this movie (p. 6)

Which genre do you expect? Collect information on the different formats and decide which genre you expect this movie to belong to.

individual solutions

Approaching *Gran Torino* (pp. 10 – 14)

1 Study the promotional poster or DVD cover of the film *Gran Torino* and tick the relevant boxes to explain whether the poster adopts the general design of movie posters.

The *Gran Torino* film poster features the movie title prominently and shows Clint Eastwood as the main actor. The prominent colors of black and brown reflect the movie's dark mood and desolate tone. The car and the gun symbolize on the one hand the main character's prized possessions and foreshadow on the other hand the theme of violence. The German version of the film poster does not contain a tagline.

2 Rank the following observations on the right in the order you became aware of them and link them on the left to the message they send.

The film poster's dark colors foreshadow the movie's focus on dramatic tension with the main protagonist prominently presented in the silhouette of Clint Eastwood, a well-known male action hero whose glare into the camera and gun in his hand suggest that he is ready to take on the challenge of protecting law and order. The car in the background as well as the type of rifle refer to past times.

3 Use the information above to write your individual analysis of the poster. Also use the vocabulary given in the following box.

See model analyses above.

A first viewing of *Gran Torino* (pp. 15 – 16)

Read the following summary of the movie. Illustrate the observations and analyses in **bold print** by using scenes from the film.

individual solutions

Analysing contents and themes of the film (pp. 16 – 17)

Here are some ideas. Tick the one which you personally find most convincing.

individual solutions: On the content level these statements are all correct.

Scene-by-scene analysis (pp. 18 ff.)

In the analysis sections, highlight words and expressions that help you characterize the two protagonists.

highlighted sections: possible solutions/highlightings.

… The ambiguity of belonging:
- more in common with his next-door neighbors than with his own spoiled-rotten family
- detachment to his family, friends, and the church

- he sees man as part of something bigger than only himself

About life and death:
- impassive and detached
- a defiant retreat from everyone and everything around him
- out there alone
- share the same neighborhood
- forge their present and future together

The funeral service:
- disgust
- isolated
- at a distance from his family
- no physical contact, no interaction
- a relic
- intransigent and grumpy, difficult to be around
- disdain
- contempt
- derision

The post-service reception at Walt's house:
- scorn
- turns down the help
- rude denial
- arrogance and revulsion
- aloofness

A celebration of life:
- parallels and differences
- people mingle
- keeps to himself
- not included

Two homes in perspective:
- 'infiltrated' the neighborhood

- do not speak the same language
- out of place
- the other as an intruder

Father Janovich calls on Walt:
- not willing to let people in his life

Thao and the Latino gang:
- two possible life paths
- withdraw into his shell

Thao and his cousin's gang:
- disoriented, used and humiliated
- close alignment with the gang

Hanging out with the guys:
- sharing an evening out together
- smiling
- relaxed
- long-time friends sharing common interests
- cheerfulness
- feels comfortable
- bonding with these men
- fortified by their friendship

The initiation rite:
- keeping their distance through ignorance and avoidance

A father-son relationship:
- barricades himself against the outer world
- insouciant and selfish
- superficial interest
- cannot count on his son
- the family does not give Walt a sense of belonging

Back to normal:
- refusing to comprise
- choosing solitude over company

Get off my lawn:
- defends his territory
- two opposing settings
- misanthropic, withdrawn and weakened
- alienated from his family
- a stranger in his neighborhood
- disconcerted
- trapped
- a common fight
- common enemies
- more mutual understanding

The hero of the neighborhood:
- approximation and similarities

Honouring Walt:
- irritated
- appeasing gestures
- listens to
- embarrassed
- seeing eye to eye
- astonishment and reflection

Back off!
- stands up to
- defiance
- courage
- abandoned
- step in
- helping
- crossed a line
- stood up for someone
- empathizing with her distress
- backs her up

A lesson in Hmong:
- asking questions

- is curious
- explaining the difference
- thoughtful
- keeps an open mind
- pleasantly surprised

Birthday presents for Walt:
- humiliated by the disrespectful behavior
- experiences the virtues and benefits of a tightly knit community
- misjudge his needs
- an infringement on his personal freedom
- enjoying each other's company
- found out but understood at the same time
- feels part of this community
- starts seeing things and people in a different light
- reaches out to
- make amends

Thao's first day:
- overcome their aversion
- recognize
- open up
- discovers
- paternal mentor
- what a father would do for his son
- see eye to eye
- face his fate alone
- spending time together
- give and take
- profitable to both
- human bonding
- reconcile differences

What now?
- mature

- self-confident
- ready to take responsibility
- find his place in life
- cycle of violence
- 'an eye for an eye'
- outcome is fatal

Redemption:
- thin line between acting out for others and self-sacrifice
- knows where he belongs
- liberation
- contentment
- face the same fate
- mutual care and solidarity
- against hopelessness, deterioration and crime
- traded his prejudice for understanding
- gained love and respect
- redeem his own past

Nothing is fair:
- back in the shadows
- vindictiveness
- resolution and remedy
- the uncompromising determination to do what is right
- redemption lies in forgiveness
- in peace
- integrity and strength
- a world in which there is less room for destructive prejudice and harmful hatred but the possibility to acknowledge the other and create a sense of belonging for everyone

Put the following stills in chronological order. What has changed in the relationship between Walt and Thao?

solution: stills 4 – 1 – 3 – 2

individual solutions

Some quotes (pp. 70 – 71)

Read the given quotes and match them to a passage of the analysis so that they exemplify or illustrate the point made.

Quote 1: Hanging out with the guys: Walt realizes that he is preoccupied with death and does not know how to describe what is important for him in life.

Quote 2: A lesson in Hmong: Sue explains to Walt what the typical biographies of Hmong teenagers in the US are like.

Quote 3: Look at that: The horoscope foreshadows Walt's decision against his own family and for the neighboring family and cynically points to Walt's self-sacrificing death.

Quote 4: Another birthday: The shaman has 'read' Walt's soul and has precisely analysed his problems – the disrespect his sons and their families show and the traumatizing experience of having to shoot a Korean boy during the war.

Quote 5: Preparations: Walt is convinced that he cannot be forgiven for having killed the Korean boy. This is why he is prepared to give his life for Thao and Sue to redeem his sin.

Quote 6: Getting to work: At first intimidated by Walt's grumpy sarcasm, Thao defiantly demands fair treatment.

Character breakdowns (pp. 80 ff.)

1 First consider the logic behind the chart. What do the bold print and the font size suggest?

The bold print and font size relate to the importance of the characters in the film. Walt and Thao are obviously the movie's main characters. Walt's sons Mitch and Steve do not have the same importance in the film; whereas Mitch is present in several scenes the viewer sees Steve only at the beginning and in the end.

2 Use the chart and the vocab below to explain how the characters correlate during the movie. Draw arrows and label them.

The chart describes the two worlds into which Walt and Thao belong.

Walt's family consists of his two sons, Mitch and Steve, and their wives and children whom he seems to despise. Rather a loner Walt does not seem to feel close to many people but he has known both Tim and Martin for some time and the latter can even be considered his friend. Father Janovich, the parish priest who feels responsible for Walt, is harshly rejected by him at first but then earns his trust. Father Janovich and Sue serve as mediators between the two worlds of Walt and Thao.

Sue is his first connection to the world of the Hmong next door. She introduces Walt to her family (her mother Vu and her grandmother Phong), her culture (explaining the role and importance of the family shaman Kor Khu) and also her brother Thao for whom Walt becomes a mentor. Her fate in the movie mirrors the mixing of ethnicities (her date is Trey, a white Caucasian) and the brutal gang reality of the American suburb which nearly destroys her.

Thao, the other main character of the movie, is a loner like Walt and feels trapped in his family. The gangs of the area bully him, in particular his cousin's (Spider) gang. His friendship with Walt saves him from a fate in crime and violence.

Character outlines (pp. 84 – 85)

1 Review scenes in which you have a particularly vivid memory of a character. Discuss some of the following criteria with a partner to gain a deeper insight into the characters.

Walt(er) Kowalski's name suggests that he has Polish origins. Shortening his first name makes it sound more American and suggests that his wife or friends would call him that way.

His lean figure, his slow and controlled movements, and his measured way of talking underline Walt's self-discipline and factual approach to things. Dressed simply in jeans and a T-shirt, chewing beef jerky and drinking beer from a can on his front porch portray him as a working-class man whose sloppy and offensive language display arrogance and show prejudice which his continual racial slurs confirm. The Gran Torino in the driveway and the rifle in the basement – both relicts from the past – characterize him as a man who has achieved what he now owns through hard work and who is ready to defend what is his, even by force. His piercing stare and reluctance to say more than absolutely necessary keep all others at bay and help to create the image of a male macho loner.

Thao's name suggests his ethnic origins and is sometimes translated as 'respectful of parents'. In his disheveled but clean appearance, his slouch and slow movements the boy's disorientation and lack of energy show. The fact that he avoids all direct eye contact underline his insecurity whereas his educated way of speaking and the irony in his words betray his intelligence and his quick-mindedness. Just like Walt he keeps his emotions to himself and prefers reading a book over spending time in the company of others.

2 How do all these aspects influence the viewer's opinion of the character?

individual solutions

The two protagonists … (pp. 86 – 91)

1 Look at the expressions in the box beneath and match them to either Walt or Thao. Think of scenes that illustrate the various aspects of their personality.

individual solutions; some expressions can be matched to both protagonists

A final evaluation (pp. 93 – 94)

Match the aspects of the analysis given on the following page to lines from the song on this page.

individual solutions

Appendix

Vocab: The Ambiguity of Belonging

parallels and differences
peaceful coexistence
cooperation
living together

a sense of belonging
mutual understanding
the opportunity for personal growth
recognition
curiousity
redemption
reconciliation
integrity
forgiveness
endurance
encouragement
confirmation
liberation
contentment
profitable to both

to empathize/show empathy
to be compassionate
to comply with others
to balance one's needs and the inclinations of others
to share common interests

to overcome isolation, loneliness
to be/feel in the right place to see value in life
to be motivated
to be at peace with oneself
to let people in one's life
to recruit sb.
to be able to meet challenges
to show persistence
to be/feel accepted
to be part of something bigger than oneself
to have sth. in common with
to be in close alignment with
to bond with
to take sb. on board
to enjoy sb.'s company
to connect with
to participate in
to reach out to
to be on the defensive
quarrelsome
to make amends
to learn to trust sb.
to take a stand for/against
to confide in
to burden sb. with
a give and take
to keep sb. company
to take responsibility for
to find one's place in life
to entrusts sb. with sth.
to be on equal terms
to act out for others
to embrace sb.'s problems

to gain the respect of sb.
to feel comfortable with sb.
to provide sb. with a sense of belonging
to become inseparable
to have interests in common
to count on sb.
to confide in sb.
to compromise with
to be in touch with
to see eye to eye with
to stand up for sb.
to back sb. up
to keep an open mind towards
to acknowledge the other

a long-time friend
an acquaintance
a peer
a mate/pal
an ally

at peace
appreciated
well taken care of
integrated in
complete
inseparable from
attached
connected to
safe and secure
accepted

to be separated from
to interfere in someone else's life
to feel detached from
to turn down help
to barricade oneself against
to shut oneself off against
to keep one's distance
to collide with
to confront sb.
to choose solitude over company
to defend one's territory
to take issue with
to emphasize the differences
to patronize sb.
to take revenge on
to be out there alone
to live up to other people's expectations

excluded from
secluded/isolated
disoriented
used
humiliated
embittered
disconcerted
insouciant
selfish
misanthropic
withdrawn
alienated from
a stranger to
trapped
offensive
hostile
at a distance
unresponsive

an exception to the rule
intruder
aloofness
rude denial of support
a constraint on
a limitation to individual freedom
the demand for conformity
superficial interest
ignorance
avoidance
contempt
disdain
scorn
defiance
bullying
retreat
distress
lack of orientation
disrespectful behavior
an infringement on sb.'s freedom
aversion
distrust
irreconcilable differences
hopelessness
deterioration
vindictiveness
retribution

Vocab: Character description

adaptable
affectionate
altruistic
ambitious
annoying
anxious
arrogant
articulate
assertive
biased
bigoted
blameless
brave
bossy
careful
careless
caring
calm
cautious
childlike
class-/status-
   conscious
committed
compassionate
complex
compliant
conceited
confident
conscientious
considerate
courageous
decent
defiant
depressed
desperate
detached
determined

devoted
disconcerted
dreamer
dutiful
efficient
egoistical
embittered
energetic
fair
faithful
focused
forgiving
frustrated
fun-loving
generous
gentle
hard-working
heavily-biased
hesitant
honest
hot-headed
imaginative
impressionable
impulsive
independent
industrious
intense
interested
ironic
jealous
judgmental
kind
laid-back
likeable
lonely
loving
loyal

manipulative
materialistic
methodical
mistrustful
morally-upright
naive
open-minded
opinionated
paranoid
passive
patient
perceptive
perfectionist
perturbed
pleasant
polite
poser
positive
professional
profound
proud
questioning
quick-tempered
radical
realistic
rebellious
reflective
relaxed
reliable
reserved
respectful
(ir)responsible
responsive
rigid
rude
sarcastic
self-confident

self-conscious
selfish
self-reliant
sensible
sensitive
serious
shrewd
shy
simple-minded
slick
smart
stable
snobbish
steadfast
strong
stubborn
superficial
successful
tender
timid
thoughtful
tireless
tolerant
touchy
troubled
trusting
understanding
unscrupulous
vain
vulnerable
warm
well-informed
wise
witty
xenophobic
youthful
zealous

Vocab: Emotional reactions

acceptance
admiration
affection
aggravation
aggression
agitation
alarm
alienation
amazement
ambivalence
amusement
anxiety
apathy
apprehension
astonishment
attraction
bitterness
bliss
boredom
compassion
confusion
contempt
delight
depression
despair
distress
domination
doubt
dread
ecstasy
elation
embarrassment

empathy
enthusiasm
envy
euphoria
excitement
exhilaration
fondness
forgiveness
fright
frustration
fury
gloom
gratitude
grief
grouchiness
guilt
happiness
hate
hatred
homesickness
hope
horror
hostility
humiliation
hysteria
insecurity
interest
jealousy
joy(fulness)
kindness
loathing
loneliness

love
manipulation
melancholy
misery
mortification
panic
paranoia
pity
pleasure
pride
quirkiness
rage
regret
remorse
resentment
revulsion
sentimentality
shame
shock
suffering
sympathy
tenseness
terror
uneasiness
unhappiness
violence
worry
wrath
yearning
zeal

The language of film from A – Z

For even more terms, go to: www.imdb.com/glossary/

ambiance	The overall mood of a scene or setting	
antagonist	The main character in conflict with the film's hero(ine), lead character or protagonist (also: bad guy, or villain)	
camera angles	camera	purpose/effect
• bird's-eye view • high angle/crane/overhead shot	positioned above	With high angle shots, the viewer looks down on the action. This makes people and objects appear smaller, less important, or even insignificant, or helps to put them into a larger context.
• low angle/below shot	positioned below	Low angles may make characters look dominant, aggressive, and threatening. If focussed on the action, they will most often create an intimidating atmosphere.
• eye-level/straight-on angle	positioned at eye-level with the viewer or one of the characters involved	Eye-level shots are the most common camera angle as they help to make the viewers feel part of the scene, as if they were confronting the person or object directly. This also makes the scene feel more 'realistic'.
• establishing shot (long or wide shot)	positioned at a distance or zoomed out so that particular objects, the location in general or characters appear relatively small in the frame	Establishing shots usually occur at the beginning of a scene (or a sequence) and help the viewer to identify the location and approximate time of the scene as a form of orientation.

• medium shot (one-/two-/three-shot)	positioned at or zoomed to a medium distance so as to show a human figure from the waist or knees up, depending on the number of people or objects in the frame	Medium shots place the focus on the action/interaction of the people in the frame.
• close-up (CU) • extreme close-up (ECU)	positioned or zoomed in to a close distance so that objects and people or certain aspects of them appear relatively large and fill the entire frame	CUs and ECUs focus attention on something and emphasize its importance; when facial expressions are in focus rather than the external action, it often makes us feel either more comfortable or extremely uncomfortable.
• insert(ed) CU	refers to a shot taken of a static object, which fills most of the frame and is inserted later during the editing process, typically between two shots of a character looking offscreen	Inserted CUs are employed to emphasize a relevant object which could easily be over-looked in the complex *mise en scène* of the shot and/or to show what a character is looking at.
• point of view shot (POV)	positioned so as to take the shot from the subjective perspective of one of the characters and usually coupled with a reaction shot	POVs are meant to show the audience the scene as if through the eyes of one of the characters.

• reaction shot	refers to a quick shot that records a character's or group's response to another character or some on-screen action or event	Reaction shots help viewers to feel more involved in the dialogue or the action.
• over-(the)-shoulder shot (OTS)	refers to a shot which records the action from behind the shoulder and/or head of one of the characters, who is usually looking in the direction of another character	OTSs help to link the characters involved in a scene by establishing their respective positions. By giving the viewers the impression that they are looking at a person or a group of people from the other person's point of view, OTSs help viewers to feel like they are actually interacting with the other character(s) in the film.
• reverse angle shot/reverse shot	refers to a shot photographed from the opposite side of a person/object to provide a different perspective	Reverse angle shots are typically used for scenes in which the focus is on the dialogue and character interaction.
camera movement		
• pan(ning)/tracking shot	camera movement from left to right (or vice versa), with the camera moving on a 'dolly' (a platform on wheels)	Panning/tracking shots are used to follow the action or to survey the overall setting. This gives viewers the feeling that they are part of the scene because they are following the action closely at eye-level.
• tilt (up or down)	camera movement upwards or downwards	A tilt can be used to emphasize the height of something, to simulate someone looking up or down or to surprise the viewers by focusing on a change.

• zoom in/out	refers to changing the framing of a shot from *wide angle* to *close-up* and vice versa	Zooming in serves to isolate a person or object from the surrounding environment and to put it into focus; zooming out is used to place something or someone within a larger context.
camera speed		
• slow motion	a technique which makes people or objects appear to be moving more slowly than normal	Slow motion in films usually builds suspense, intensifies emotions or simply highlights the importance of the moment.
• fast motion	a technique which makes people or objects appear to be moving more quickly than normal	Fast motion usually creates a comic and/or hectic effect.
• freeze frame	a frame image created by stopping the film in the middle of the action	Freeze frames are often used at the end of a film to indicate death, to introduce ambiguity, and to provide an iconic, lasting image.
cast	all of the actors appearing in a film	
credits	list of cast, crew, and other people involved in making a film (*opening credits* appear at the beginning, *closing credits* at the end)	
crew	all those involved in the technical production of a film, who are not actual performers	
critic	a person who publishes a review of a film, considering it from either an artistic or entertainment point of view	
cut	an essential part of the editing process; an abrupt change in camera angle, location or time, from one shot to another	

• cross-cutting	editing technique that combines two scenes or events by alternating between them or interweaving them with one another	Cross-cutting enables viewers to realize that the two actions are somehow linked, and the characters from the different lines of action are connected in some way.
• dissolve, burn-in/-out fade-in/-out	the visible image of one shot or scene is gradually replaced, superimposed or blended in or out (by an overlapping fade-out or fade-in and following dissolve) of the image from another shot or scene	This superimposition of shots is often used to suggest the passage of time or to imitate hallucinatory states.
• match cut	a cut between two shots (outgoing and incoming), which are felt to be 'matched' because they contain similar elements	A match cut emphasizes the continuity of the action and helps to link one scene to another more smoothly.
director	a director usually has the complete artistic control over all aspects of the film, such as casting, script editing, shot selection, shot composition, and editing, etc. On the film set, the director is also responsible for communicating to actors how a particular scene is to be performed.	
editing	the process by which the many separate camera takes of the filming process are selected, assembled, arranged, trimmed, structured, and spliced (= joined) together to form a complete sequence in line with the script	

eyeline	the direction in which a character is looking	Eyelines are often a way of letting the viewers know what (or whom) a character is interested in.
focus	refers to the degree of sharpness and clarity in a film image; 'out-of-focus': images are blurred and lack clear linear definition	
foreshadowing	refers to hints provided within a film (in the form of symbols, images, motifs, repetition, dialogue or mood) about the outcome of the plot, or about an upcoming action that will take place	This is often done in order to prepare viewers for later events, revelations, or plot developments; ominous music also often foreshadows danger or builds suspense.
frame	a single image of a film	
interior/exterior	a scene apparently shot indoors or out of doors	
lighting	refers to the overall illumination of the set and may be described in terms of the direction from which the light enters the set (front-lighting, back-lighting, side-lighting, top-lighting, cross-lighting) or simply in terms of the contrast between light and dark (high-key, low-key lighting)	
mise en scène	refers to all of the elements within the frame of the film and how they are arranged in front of the camera; includes, for example, the setting, overall decor, props, actors, costumes, makeup, lighting, performances and characters	

Index

Acknowledgements

Texts

p. 93: "Gran Torino"; text and music: James Cullum, Clint Eastwood, Kyle C. Eastwood, Michael C. Stevens, *The Pursuit*, 2009; EMI Music Publishing Ltd./EMI Music Publishing Germany GmbH; https://www.songtexte.com/songtext/jamie-cullum/gran-torino-33e0e899.html [24.01.2019]

Pictures

|alamy images, Abingdon/Oxfordshire: Wiener, Mark 1, 55. |Domke, Franz-Josef, Hannover: 6. |Shutterstock.com (RM), New York: BEI/REX 5; Warner Bros/Kobal/REX 10, 41, 48, 49. |Warner Bros. Entertainment Inc., Burbank/California: Gran Torino. Regie: Clint Eastwood, Darsteller (v. l. n. r.): Bee Vang, Clint Eastwood. Warner Bros Pictures 2009. 49; Gran Torino. Regie: Clint Eastwood, Darsteller (v. l. n. r.): Christopher Carley, Brian Haley, Dreama Walker, Geraldine Hughes, Dreama Walker, Clint Eastwood. Warner Bros Pictures 2009 23; Gran Torino. Regie: Clint Eastwood, Darsteller (v. l. n. r.): Clint Eastwood, Bee Vang. Warner Bros Pictures 2009 48; Gran Torino. Regie: Clint Eastwood, Darsteller (v. l. n. r.): Cory Hardrict, Ahney Her, Nana Gbewonyo, Clint Eastwood. Warner Bros Pictures 2009 41; Gran Torino. Regie: Clint Eastwood, Darsteller: Bee Vang. Warner Bros Pictures 2009 29; Gran Torino. Regie: Clint Eastwood, Darsteller: Clint Eastwood. Warner Bros Pictures 2009 65.